HEADED UPSTREAM

HEADED UPSTREAM

INTERVIEWS
WITH
ICONOCLASTS

BY
JACK LOEFFLER

HARBINGER HOUSE
TUCSON

Frontispiece: Jack Loeffler with Edward Abbey.

Harbinger House, Inc.
3131 N. Country Club, Suite 106
Tucson, Arizona 85716

This book was set in Trump Mediaeval with Avant Garde
Display
Designed by Paul Mirocha

Photo credits: p. ii—Katherine Loeffler; p. 2, 88, 100—Terrence
Moore; pp. 20, 32, 44, 58, 68, 78, 112, 128, 138, 148, 158, 166,
176—Jack Loeffler; p. 94—Paul Mirocha; pp. 172, 188—
George Grant (courtesy National Park Service, Museum
Collections Repository Archives, Tucson, Arizona)

Library of Congress Cataloging in Publication Data

Loeffler, Jack, 1936–
    Headed upstream : interviews with iconoclasts / by Jack
    Loeffler.
        p. cm.
    ISBN 0-943173-21-3 : $10.95
        1. Human ecology—Interviews. 2. Human ecology—
    Philosophy. 3. Ethnophilosophy. 4. Indians of North
    America—Philosophy. I. Title.
    GF21.L63 1989 304.2—dc20 89-35707

To Ed,
Clarke,
Susie,
Becky,
and
Ben Abbey

CONTENTS

PREFACE

THE ROLE of the oral historian is to poke microphones through rents in the mesh of monoculture, to seek sources of provocative sound and select that which is relevant to record. Amidst the white noise generated by a planetary human population of over five billion, one may still discern certain sounds of great natural beauty: the mellifluous, downward-slurring song of the canyon wren, the deep-throated hawking of sandhill cranes, the warbling of water awash in a side canyon, the poignant howl of the Mexican wolf.

For a quarter of a century now I have wandered along an endless trail, packing a tape recorder, a notebook, pens and my kit, listening, recording, asking questions, and frequently communicating with fellow humans and other creatures with whom I share no common language. Sometimes I record for hire, but mostly I follow my own inclinations and trust to the inspiration of the moment. I have recorded many miles of music, often of an indigenous or traditional suchness. I have listened in on myriad sounds which emanate from the flow of Nature.

At various times I have regarded myself as an oral historian, a sound recordist, a field ethnomusicologist, a documentarian, a radio journalist, a filmmaker, a musician, a writer. I have been frustrated by the narrowness of the slots to which one can be relegated. For the time being, I regard myself as an oral historian, a title nebulous enough to allow some latitude.

In a time when mass media and the music industry dominate much of the attention of monoculture, the onus is on the oral historian to search out those who live within coordinates of their own calculation, and who sometimes regard the culturally acceptable as contemptible. The archive of an oral historian who has been active for many years contains thousands of sounds that may be revealed to be curiously related.

My own interest in oral history began in the early 1960s when I became an ardent advocate of preserving native, or indigenous, cultures. I had long felt that Christian missionaries and government-sponsored educators presumed greatly at the expense of Indian peoples whose cosmologies and life-styles were far richer and much more respectful of the natural world—less exploitative and anthropocentric—than those of the people who would dominate them. To pass through the Indian country of the American Southwest in the days before massive mineral extraction was to experience the song of the mythic landscape where the Navajos focused their attention on walking in beauty and the Puebloans performed endless cycles of ceremonials that celebrate the eternal dance of the deities.

Even then, however, any Navajo who entered a Bureau of Indian Affairs school on the reservation was greeted by the iniquitous slogan within that artlessly declared, "Tradition is the enemy of progress." Progress into a religious system where reverence for an icon allegedly exonerates one from individual responsibility by an act of faith? Progress into a state of technofantasy[1] that tolls the knell for mythic processes which have sustained hearty cultures in harmony with their environment for millennia?

---

1. Technofantasy is a state of mind where human attention is externalized and focused on the process and product of human invention. In Western culture technofantasy has resulted in many ramifications including rampant extraction of natural resources, widespread pollution of natural environment, and a form of cultural preoccupation with inorganic trivia.

As it became apparent that indigenous cultures were endangered, I began my wandering into the most remote inhabited areas of the American Southwest and Mexico. I lived with Navajos and Huicholes. I got to know Tarahumaras, Hopis, Utes, Yakimas, Papagos, Pimas, Puebloans, Sioux, Apaches, Washos, and Paiutes. I began to conduct interviews and came to realize the extent to which language casts the way one thinks—that indeed people from different linguistic phyla may believe they share common denominators which they actually do not. Human conduct is definitely open to interpretation, and the world wanderer may remain aghast until he thoroughly understands the degree to which mores are phenomena of culture held in place by oral tradition. Mores are a means of interpreting reality from within a cultural continuum.

As the decade of the '60s wore on, I spent more and more time in the woods or way out in the desert—anywhere I felt that I was beyond the pale of western culture. I reveled in the range of feelings and emotions one experiences walking naked beneath the sun, listening to the pulse of the Earth. And I discovered that even though one may be born into a system under the influence of a goety of industriogogues and their men in government, one may regain a healthy state of mind, and experience first hand a perception of the interrelatedness of it all. I sensed what, to me, is verbally inexpressible. I perceived the sense of place within the place; nonhuman Life and the energy that melds the molecules of stones and stars became overwhelmingly sacred to me. I fell wildly in love with the Earth. I still am.

I must admit that I am not exempt from continuing to rely on my pickup truck to haul me, my tape recorder to support me, good books to sustain me, and my family and friends to be my family and friends. I remain affiliated.

I have recorded a great deal that has its genesis in western monoculture. And eastern monoculture. The ping-pong paddles of interracial competition. Net gain, net loss, net gain, net loss etc. I have recorded unnatural sound, but I have my limits.

As I've traveled I've had the good fortune to meet and frequently befriend people whose minds have evolved beyond the mean imposed by advertising and commercial entertainment—people whose thinking runs counter to the current of the continuum, people of ideas and fortitude. I greatly admire humans who assume responsibility for their own thinking and rely little on the alleged miracle of modern technofantasy to successfully industrialize survival. I also admire those who respect and defend the rights of both individuals and indigenous cultures to evolve as they will, and would thwart exploiters and mineral bandits, be they from East or West. And I unconditionally support any who tangle with bureaucracies manned by maintenance personnel who lubricate and tend a juggernaut that relentlessly strips our planet of her *elan vital*, and spreads unreined, even though there are those who believe themselves to reign. (The word "juggernaut" is thought to have come from the name of the Hindu god Jagannath, who is an aspect of the Lord Vishnu. In ritual an enormous icon supported by a chariot was drawn by thousands of worshipers, many of whom would throw themselves beneath the chariot in a frenzy of religious ecstasy and be crushed by the omnipotent Jagannath.)

This book contains interviews with people who express ideas and concepts that buck the juggernaut, slide in from the oblique angle, or otherwise pique the poise of the contented. Everyone in this book has stood naked, in a way, before the barrage of criticism that inevitably falls upon innovative ideas or deeds that run against the tide.

Most of the interviews presented herein—Ed Abbey, Garrett Hardin, Godfrey Reggio, Andy Weil, Anna Sofaer, Alvin Josephy, John Nichols, Dave Foreman, Doug Peacock, John Fife, Gary De-Walt, Philip Whalen and Gary Snyder—were originally conducted for a radio series I produced which was funded by the New Mexico Arts Division. The series is entitled *Southwest Sound Collage* and was distributed to public radio stations around the United States beginning in 1986. "A Traditional Hopi Perspective" is an article based on interviews conducted in the kiva at Hotevilla, Hopi Independent Nation, in 1971. This article appeared in *Myths & Technofantasies*, *Not Man Apart* and *Clear Creek*. "Monster in Dinetah" was produced by a grant from the University of New Mexico and has been distributed to public radio stations around the United States by the Pacifica Radio Archive in Los Angeles. The interview with Stewart Udall became the basis for a radio program entitled "Black Mesa Sacrifice" and was broadcast over National Public Radio in 1986.

I liken this book to a series of chord progressions wherein certain themes—environmental ethics and defense, human values maintained by traditional cultures, contemporary anarchist thought—become the leitmotifs which comprise the whole composition.

At any rate, when I conducted and recorded these interviews, it was music to my ears.

Jack Loeffler
Osprey Bay,
Sea of Cortez

ACKNOWLEDGMENTS

I WISH TO SAY THANKS to the many people who helped this book into being, including all of the interviewees, the old gang at the Black Mesa Defense Fund, Jimmy Hopper, Terry Moore, Katherine Loeffler, Karl Kernberger, Bill Brown (who invented the word "technofantasy"), Phil Shultz, Brant Calkin, Harvey Mudd, John Kimmey, Caroline Rackley, Hannah Hibbs, Tom Andrews, Preston Bell, Trisha Stanton, Jean Green, Peggy Swift, Joe Brecher, Richard Clemmer, Dan Budnik, Jerry Mander, Pennfield Jensen, Melissa Savage, David Padwa, Celestia Peregrina Loeffler, John DePuy, Gordon Ashby, Stewart Brand, Jonathan Altman, Thomas and Fermina Banyacya, Dave Brower, the Native American Rights Fund, Huey Johnson, Pete Seeger, Don MacLean, Dennis Hopper, Richard Grow and the Big Mountain Support Group in Berkeley, the Hog Farm, Susanne Jamison, the New Mexico Arts Division, Anne Weaver, Polly Rose, Zdenek Gerych, Ken Nichols, Bahi, Roberta Blackgoat, Ninebah, the spirits of Mina Lansa, David Monongye, and John Lansa, and the memory of Peter Kropotkin, who contended that mutual cooperation is at least as important a factor in the evolution of species as mutual antagonism.

HEADED UPSTREAM

EDWARD ABBEY

EDWARD ABBEY LEFT IN HIS WAKE a legacy of literature that shows the mind of the master, which has inspired a generation of individualists to react in behalf of this biotic entity we know as the planet Earth. He was undeniably a radical environmentalist. His literary presence evoked a wave of awakening to the enormous jeopardy imposed on the natural environment of the American Southwest by an overabundance of fellow humans.

Ed produced a score of books, including Desert Solitaire, The Brave Cowboy, Black Sun, Good News, The Monkey Wrench Gang, One Life at a Time, Please, *and what he regarded as his "fat classic,"* The Fool's Progress. *Days before he was last seen wandering west into the sun, he finished the first draft of* Hayduke Lives!, *his sequel to* The Monkey Wrench Gang.

Ed was as close a friend as I'll have in this lifetime. We went on dozens of camping trips and walked hundreds, maybe thousands, of miles talking about everything under the sun and the moon. We floated rivers and kept each other's secrets. Once we had a wreck out in the middle of somewhere. Ours were the only two pickup trucks within hundreds of square miles and sure enough, we ran into each other. When Ed emerged from the cab of his pickup leaking blood out of a cut over his eye, I laughed so hard I damn near fainted.

Someone recently told me that there are those who regarded Abbey as a man filled with rage. I'll never believe this. Ed told me that the only time he could condone the use of personal violence would be in defense of his loved ones. I know that his love extended beyond his family and friends to include empty spaces, wilderness, all living creatures. What he detested was everything that degraded life—bureaucracy, mineral extractors, the military-industrial-governmental complex, developers— against these ubiquitous agents of antilife he bore within him a great anger. If he committed acts of sabotage he did so in behalf of life. He was careful to differentiate between terrorism and sabotage. To him the distinction was simple enough. Terrorism is violence against life—bombing passenger planes, strafing Vietnamese villages, strip-mining the earth. Conversely, sabotage is the disabling of the machinery of terrorism.

Ed Abbey celebrated life. In a way he was a mystic and a hermit. He was also a husband, a father and a true friend. If indeed there was rage in Edward Abbey, it was a rage to live and be conscious, to love and to follow the truth no matter where it led.

On our last trip together, just before he headed down a trail forbidden to the living, we looked each other in the eye and said "so long." I asked him what he wanted for an epitaph. He grinned and said, "No comment."

———

JACK LOEFFLER   Could you define the way you regard reality in this latter part of the twentieth century, the way the United States of America is functioning?

EDWARD ABBEY   Unhuh, very serious. Makes me think of James Joyce saying that history is a nightmare from which he is trying to awake. Or as Saul Bellow said, "History is a nightmare in which I'm trying to get a good night's sleep." But here goes: I think human beings have made a nightmare out of their collective history. Seems to me that the last 5,000 years have been pretty awful—cruelty, slavery, torture, religious fanaticism, ideological fanaticisms, the old serfdom of agriculture and the new serfdom of industrialism. I think humankind probably made a big mistake when we gave up the hunting and gathering way of life for agriculture. Ever since then the majority of us have led the lives of slaves and dependents. I look forward to the time when the industrial system collapses and we all go back to chasing wild cattle and buffalo on horseback.

I think the human race has become a plague upon this Earth. There are far too many of us making too many demands on one defenseless little planet. Human beings have as much right to be here as any other animal, but we have abused that right by allowing our numbers to grow so great and our appetites to become so gross that we are plundering the earth and destroying most other forms of life, threatening our own survival by greed and stupidity and this insane mania for quantitative growth, for perpetual expansion, the desire for domination over nature and our fellow humans.

The wilderness is vanishing. Next to go will be the last primitive tribes, the traditional cultures that still survive in places like the Far North and the African and South American tropics. And if the whole planet becomes industrialized, technologized, urbanized, that would be almost the worst disaster that can befall the planet and human beings. I think it would lead to the ultimate techno-tyranny that some of our better science fiction writers have prophesied.

I think by virtue of reason, common sense, the evidence of our five good bodily senses and daily experience, we can imagine a better way to live, with fairly simple solutions. Not easy—but simple. Beginning here in America—we should set the example. We have set the example for pillaging the planet and we should set the example for preserving life, including human life. First, most important, reduce human numbers, gradually, by normal attrition, letting the senile old farts like you and me die off. Reduce the human population to a reasonable number, a self-sustaining number—for the United States something like 100 million, or even 50 million should be plenty. And then, second, simplify our needs and demands, so that we're not preying to excess on other forms of life—plant life and animal life—by developing new attitudes, a natural reverence for all forms of life.

I consider myself an absolute egalitarian. I think that all human beings are essentially equal, deserve equal regard and consideration. Certainly everyone differs in ability. Some people are bigger, stronger; some are smarter; some are more clever with their hands; others are more clever with their brains. There's an infinite variation in talent and ability and intelligence among individual humans, but I think that all, except the most depraved, violently criminally insane—generals and dictators—are of equal value. There's another basis for this kind of egalitarianism. Just by virtue of being alive, we deserve to be respected as individuals. Furthermore, that respect for the value of each human being should be extended to each living thing on the planet, to our fellow creatures, beginning with our pet dogs and cats and horses. Humans find it easy to love them. We can and must learn to love the wild animals, the mountain lions and the rattlesnakes and the coyotes, the buffalo and the elephants, as we do our pets. And developing that way, extend our ability to love to include plant life. A tree, a shrub, a blade of grass, deserves respect and sympathy as fellow living things.

I think you can go even beyond that to respect the rocks, the air, the water. Because each is part of a whole—each part dependent on the other parts. If only for our own self-respect and survival, we can learn to love the world around us—go beyond the human and love the nonhuman. Instead of simply trying to dominate, subjugate, enslave it, as we've been doing for the last 5,000 years, learn to live in some sort of harmony with it. Use what we must use; all living creatures have to feed on other living creatures. but do it at a reasonable level, so that other things can also survive. I guess Albert Schweitzer was right when he said, "We must learn reverence for all forms of life," even those we have to hunt, kill and eat. Especially those.

JL How do you consider dwelling with those who are antagonistic to life?

EA I think in the long run that life will destroy them. The destroyers are destroyed—the dictators and the militarists. In the meantime, though, we've got to teach our children sympathy for life and all living things. That begins as an individual, personal responsibility—develop this love for life in ourselves, try to pass it on to our children, try to spread it beyond the family as far as we can by whatever means are available. Teachers, writers, artists, scientists, performers, politicians have the primary obligation. A good politician is one with the ability to lead people toward this attitude. It's hard to think of any such.

JL When it becomes apparent that we're not gaining philosophically fast enough in the wake of big business and political maneuvering, what steps do you think are justifiable in trying to turn the tide that seems to lead, literally, to a dead end, not just for our species, but the whole planet?

EA I suppose if political means fail us—public organization and public pressure—if those don't do what has to be done, then we'll be driven to more extreme defensive measures in defending our

Earth. Here in the United States, I can see a lot more acts of civil disobedience beginning to occur, as the bulldozers and the drilling rigs attempt to move into the wilderness and into the back country and the farmlands and seashores and other precious places. And if civil disobedience is not enough, I imagine there will be sabotage, violence against machinery, property. Those are desperate measures. If they become widespread, it could be that the battle has already been lost. I don't know what would happen beyond that. Such resistance might stimulate some sort of police-state reaction, repression, a real military-industrial dictatorship in this country.

But still, personally, I feel that when all other means fail, we are morally justified—not merely justified, but morally obligated—to defend that which we love by whatever means are available. Just as, if my family, my life, my children were attacked, I wouldn't hesitate to use violence to defend them. By the same principle, if land I love is being violated, raped, plundered, murdered, and all political means to save it have failed, I personally feel that sabotage is morally justifiable. At least, if it does any good, if it'll help. If it will only help you to feel good . . .

JL   I would hazard that some would call acts of physical sabotage "terrorism."

EA   The distinction is quite clear and simple. Sabotage is an act of force or violence against material objects, machinery, in which life is not endangered, or should not be. Terrorism, on the other hand, is violence against living things—human beings and other living things. That kind of terrorism is generally practiced by governments against their own peoples. We have that kind of terrorism going on right now in much of Latin America— Guatemala, El Salvador, and quite recently in Argentina and Chile, and a mild form of it in Poland during the past year. The Soviets are committing terrorism against the people of Afghanistan right now—with limited success, I'm happy to hear. Our government committed great acts of terrorism against the people of Vietnam. That's what terrorism means—violence and threat of violence against human beings and other forms of life. Which is radically different from sabotage, a much more limited form of conflict. I'd go so far as to say that a bulldozer tearing up a hillside, ripping out trees for a logging operation or a strip mine is committing terrorism—violence against life.

JL   For a long time you've been regarded as . . .

EA   A real swine—I get a lot of hate mail, which I'm very proud of.

JL   But you've been regarded as a real defender of the West. Could you talk a little bit about the different faces of jeopardy which the West is experiencing right now?

EA   The different faces of jeopardy? Great phrase, great phrase. What the hell does it mean? Actually, I've done most of my defending of the West with a typewriter, which is an easy and cowardly way to go about it. I most respect those who are activists, at least in this area of human life—people like Dave Brower and Dave Foreman, to name only two. There are thousands of people involved in conservation, thousands, and they should all be named, if it were possible—the people who actually carry on the fight, who do the difficult work of organizing public resistance, who do the lobbying and the litigating, the buttonholing of Congressmen, or in some cases, who run for public office, who draw petitions and circulate them, who do the tedious office work and paperwork that have to be done to save what's left of America. I respect those people very much. I respect them much more than people who merely sit behind a desk and write about it.

JL   What do you think is the Southwest's biggest enemy right now?

EA   Oh, the same old thing—expansion, development, commercial greed, industrial growth. That kind of growth which has become a pathological condition in our society. That insatiable demand for more and more; the urge to dominate and consume

9

and destroy. The rangelands overgrazed and the hills being strip-mined and the rivers being dammed and the farmlands eroded and the air, soil and water being poisoned in the usual, various ways—just the endless speeding up of this process and the expansion of its territory. The whole West is being gradually destroyed by this corporate greed. Not to mention the rest of the world.

JL   It's possible to see what motivates those without any sense of environmental integrity, who are really motivated by the desire for power and money. But what about the Joe Sixpacks of the world who operate the bulldozers? Do you think it's possible to define a characteristic in the human animal that causes this blind pillaging? Where do you think the problem lies?

EA   I do not think it lies with the Joe Sixpacks. I've been a Joe Sixpack for much of my life—had to work various jobs, most of them rather tedious, simply to get by, make a living. No, I certainly don't blame working people. They're more victimized by this process than the rest of us. Most of them have their lives and their health threatened more directly and more constantly, simply by the work they do, than we lucky ones who escaped that trap.

But where, how, did the disease begin? It really does seem to me like a kind of cancer, a tumor on human society. I would say it began when we gave up the traditional hunting and gathering way of life, and made the terrible mistake of settling down to agriculture. Somebody said that the plough may have done more damage to human life on the planet than the sword. I'd be inclined to agree.

Then agriculture was followed by industrialism, which began only about 200 years ago, as a result of the new way of looking at the world invented by a few European philosophers and scientists a century earlier. They discovered the means, the ability, to achieve mastery over nature. And here we come back to human nature again. Once we discover we have the ability to push things around, or to push other people around, most humans do not have the self-control to refrain from using such power. "Power corrupts," as some wise man said. "And absolute power corrupts absolutely." Science and technology give us absolute power over the rest of life, including human life. And power not only corrupts, it attracts the worst elements of the human herd. Power attracts the worst men and corrupts the best.

Humans have always wanted to achieve some sort of control over their environment—not only the moderns, but the most ancient tribes practiced magic and ritual in the effort to bring things under control for the perfectly honorable purpose of surviving. But somehow, in the last 5,000 years, this normal, natural, healthy, wholesome desire to survive and continue human life and raise a family and pass your genes on to succeeding generations has been corrupted by the desire to dominate, to achieve power. And we began by enslaving one another.

The first industrial systems, really, were those of Egypt, Mesopotamia, and ancient China, where thousands, or hundreds of thousands, or millions, were conscripted into work gangs of one sort or another to build huge monuments to the glory of some tyrant—the pyramids of Egypt, the Great Wall of China. Society itself became a kind of machine, as Lewis Mumford has pointed out. The original megamachines were made of human bodies—flesh and bone—human slavery. That was the true original sin. And for thousands of years since, our society has depended on the enslavement of humans—either simple chattel slavery like that of the blacks in America, or the slightly more subtle form of serfdom in Europe—the peasants and the lords and that new form of slavery we call wage slavery—chaining people to routine tasks, whether in a factory, a store, an office—compelling them to perform tedious, stupid, repetitive work in order to eat. And even when the slaves are well paid, living in suburban houses with thousands of dollars worth of gadgets and a car and a pickup truck and a motorboat, they are still slaves to the system. Most of us are slaves. We are dependent upon the industrial machine.

We cannot break free from it. We have to support it and work for it or be cut off and starve. That is slavery—a debased and degrading life without independence, without freedom.

So it began; we enslaved the horse; we created the mule; made slaves of dogs. Soon afterwards we learned to enslave human beings. Now, today, our technological-industrial social machine is trying to enslave the whole of Nature—put *everything* to work for the sake of human greed and human power. That I think is the great evil, the ultimate evil, of the modern age. By "modern" I mean of course the last 5,000 years, when the nightmare of history began.

JL   The concept of slavery in the sense of submission to domination has had a tremendous effect on the last of the so-called traditional peoples, the indigenous peoples who still inhabit the Southwestern landscape—specifically the Puebloans and the Navajos and the Papagos and the Pimas. Please give your thoughts and feelings with regard to the acculturation of these people. What can we learn from these people, if anything, to incorporate into our own culture?

EA   I think the best thing we could do for the traditional people is to let them bloody well alone—keep our greedy hands off their land and off their lives. If only that were possible. But most of them now are shut up in little enclaves within the industrial society, and most of them have become so corrupted by our society that they have become dependent upon it. So it appears to me that there are very few genuinely traditional cultures left— perhaps a few tribes down in the Amazonian jungle that still lead self-reliant lives. Maybe in New Guinea and the distant hills of the Philippines. But the American Indians have been almost totally assimilated into our culture. I realize there are a few pockets of the traditional culture still left on the reservations, but they are a small and diminishing minority, not likely to survive much longer.

Ideally, I would say we should declare the Papago Reservation, for example, and the Navajo Reservation to be fully independent nations and try to simply let them alone. But it's too late for that. It couldn't possibly work. The world has become too interdependent now. Somehow the Papagos and the Navajos, to name only those two tribes, are going to have to work out a decent life for themselves within American society. It seems to me that the majority of them are facing the same difficulties that the rest of us white Americans are facing, and the blacks and the Hispanics—how to survive in a crackpot economy, a crazy industrial empire, that the managers cannot manage and the economists cannot comprehend. Most of the American Indians have been reduced to the role of unemployed working people. Redskinned rednecks. Part of the so-called "underclass."

I would love to see the traditional cultures survive, but unless our industrial economy collapses in the near future, I don't think they will. Take the Tarahumara of Mexico. I was last down there in the Sierra Madres about ten years ago, and even then the Tarahumara way of life was clearly being threatened, constricted, closed in upon by massive road-building schemes, by heavy logging in the mountains that's bound to erode those tiny little milpas, those little corn patches down in the canyons that the Tarahumaras used to depend on—maybe still do. Even then a lot of them had been reduced to the role of pandering to tourists, selling trinkets to the passing tourist trade. They're in a bad situation. Their chances for survival as a culture are not good. No doubt they'll survive as human beings—their chances to keep on living and reproducing are about as good as the rest of us. But as tribes, coherent cultures, they don't seem to be able to compete very well in this mad rat race that most of us are dedicated to. And in order to compete successfully, they would have to abandon most of their traditional culture. They would have to become ambitious, pushing, get their kids into college and see to it that they graduate and take up the dreary trades of computer taping and programming and manufacturing that most Americans are already condemned to. I don't think a traditional culture can survive when it's surrounded by a modern, aggressive, expanding industrial culture. I wish it could. There's much we could learn from traditional peoples, and already have learned from them, but are not using.

Much has been written about this, of course—tons of books. And most of us lament the passing of the old American Indian way of life. We romanticize it and glorify it, now that it's mostly gone. Myself, I think I would have loved to have been a 19th century—early 19th century—Sioux or Arapahoe of Cheyenne, part of that great, magnificent horse-taming, buffalo-hunting way of life. The Indians of the plains, for a brief two or three centuries, had a wonderful way of life, based on the horse and the buffalo; self-reliant tribes living a self-sustaining way of life. It could probably have continued for thousands of years, if European culture had not come along and destroyed it.

JL   How would you compare the integrity of the deities of the Indians of this continent with the deities which have guided white Anglo-Saxon Protestant culture to its current point in time?

EA   Oh, like many other people, I regard the invention of monotheism and the other-worldly God as a great setback for human life. Maybe even worse than the invention of agriculture. Once we took the gods out of nature, out of the hills and forests around us and made all those little gods into one great god up in the sky, somewhere in outer space, why about then human beings, particularly Europeans, began to focus our attention on transcendental values, a transcendental deity, which led to a corresponding contempt for nature and the world which feeds and supports us. From that point of view, I think the Indians and most traditional cultures had a much wiser world view, in that they invested every aspect of the world around them—all of nature—animal life, plant life, the landscape itself, with gods, with deity. In other words, everything was divine in some way or another. Pantheism probably led to a much wiser way of life, more capable of surviving over long periods of time. The American Indian culture lasted at least 20,000 years here in North America before the Europeans destroyed it. And although it supported only a relatively small population, maybe five million, maybe ten million, nobody really knows, it lasted a long time. Our European-American-Japanese industrial culture is now about 200 years old, and it's supporting huge populations—billions—but it seems doubtful that it can survive for more than another century or two—unless there's a drastic change in our way of life.

More and more, as I said before, we try to solve our problems by submitting to some sort of technological rationalization, which includes the expansion of the industrial system onto the moon and the rest of the galaxy and god knows where. No wonder all the bodies in the heavenly universe seem to be flying away from planet Earth, according to some astronomers. They're trying to flee this plague of domination and greed. Which is also, paradoxically, the glory of our race. I admire the adventure of it. I'm in favor of space exploration, for example. I admire science and scientists, insofar as their purpose is to advance knowledge, to learn about the world we live in. If somehow we could keep our knowledge separated from our itch to dominate and tyrannize and enslave, I think science would be almost entirely a good thing. But instead, science has been largely misapplied for war and industrialism and thus has done far more harm than good, so far. Even so, I respect and admire the intellectual adventure of science: one of the great achievements of European-American humankind. Where were we? What were we talking about?

JL We just finished off the local deity.

EA Call me a pantheist. If there is such a thing as divinity, and the holiness is all, then it must exist in everything, and not simply be localized in one supernatural figure beyond time and space. Either everything is divine, or nothing is. All partake of the universal divinity—the scorpion and the packrat, the Junebug and the pismire, and even human beings. All or nothing, now or never, here and now.

JL   From a political point of view . . .

EA   I'm a registered anarchist.

JL   How long have you been a registered anarchist?

EA   Five thousand years. In practical politics, day-to-day politics, I consider myself a liberal democrat. But in the realm of ideal politics, I'm some sort of agrarian, barefoot, wilderness, eco-freak anarchist. One of my favorite thinkers is Prince Kropotkin. Another is Henry Thoreau.

JL   About ten years ago, you gave me a copy of George Woodcock's *Anarchism*. You actually wrote one of your theses on it.

EA   My only thesis.

JL   When did you write that?

EA   Oh, back in the '50s, mid-'50s at the University of New Mexico, after I flunked out of Edinburgh, Scotland, and got kicked out of Yale after two weeks, I came back . . . crawled back to New Mexico and very humbly wrote a little master's thesis for the philosophy department there. Which started out as an ambitious project—it was going to be a general theory of anarchism. The thesis committee and professors soon condensed it to a tiny little historical study of a few 19th century anarchist writers, like Prudhon, Kropotkin and Bakunin, so it ended up, like most master's theses, being nothing but a monograph on a very limited subject—namely, the ethics and morality of violence as a political method. Everything phrased in quite a circumspect manner, bristling with footnotes, half of it consisting of bibliography and notes. And thus I became a Master of Arts, a degree which means absolutely nothing.

JL   Could you talk about the stages of life in a man, and the way you have regarded your own life as a way to live them?

EA   I wish I could quote for you the seven stages of life as described by Shakespeare. He summed it up pretty well, from mewling, puking infant to beslippered, slobbering, senile old man.

That's the course most of us are foredoomed to follow. But, ideally again, I think a man's life should progress from a wild, crazy, adventurous youth through a sedate and domesticated middle age, in which we perform our biological functions of reproducing (to a modest extent; these days none of us should have more than one child); going from middle age into a free, liberated and contemplative old age in which we should have something to teach the younger generations—but only if they come around and ask. Teach, not preach.

Nothing's sorrier than an old man who has nothing to say, nothing to tell us, no advice or wisdom to offer. A young man should be an adventurer. A middle-aged man should be a producer of useful goods for his fellow humans, a good husband to a wife, and father of children. And an old man should again be an adventurer, not physical as in youth, but an adventurer in ideas. And if he learns anything from life he should be not only willing but able to teach what he's learned to those who have sense enough to want to learn something. If they can find an old man who has ability enough to teach them anything. Which is the way the traditional cultures got by for about a million years. That's something we seem in danger of losing in our culture— the old folks are simply discarded, kicked aside into nursing homes or Airstream trailers—well-supported, most of them, but largely neglected. Must I add that what I said of men, young men, middle-aged men and old men, applies with equal force to women? They too must go through the three great stages in order to live a full human life. And if you can live a full human life, that should be the life abundant for anyone. It should be sufficient.

An adventurous human life should be enough for anybody, and should free us from the childish hankering for personal immortality. Which of us is worthy to live forever, eternally? Nobody I know. And what's the point of it anyway? If this life here and now on this splendid planet we call Earth is not good enough for us, then what possible pleasure or satisfaction or happiness could we find in some sort of transcendental, eternal existence beyond time and space? Eternity, in that sense, beyond time, could be nothing but a moment, a flash, and we probably experience that brilliant flash of eternity at the moment of death. Then we should get the hell out of the way, with our bodies decently planted in the earth to nourish other forms of life—weeds, flowers, shrubs, trees, which support other forms of life, which support the ongoing human pageant—the lives of our children. That seems good enough to me.

Now, maybe when I become a terrified old man, I will dig out the Bible again and start babbling about a life beyond the grave. I think the desire for immortality is based on fear. On a terrible fear of dying, fear of death, which comes from not having fully lived. If your life has been wasted, then naturally you're going to hate giving it up. If you've led a cowardly, or paltry or tedious or uneventful life, then as you near the end of it, you're going to cling like a drowning man to whatever kind of semi-life medical technology can offer you, and you're going to end up in a hospital with a dozen tubes sticking in your body; machines keeping your organs going. Which is the worst possible way to die. Better by far to fall off a rock while climbing a cliff, or to die in battle.

JL   Can you conceive of a situation where it would be possible for a person with a terminal disease to use his or her body as a weapon in a battle?

EA   I look forward to the day when somebody with a terminal disease (such as life) is going to strap a load of TNT around his waist and go down in the bowels of Glen Canyon dam and blow that ugly thing to smithereens. That would be a good way to go.

I think one should live honorably and die honorably. One's death should mean something. One should try to have a good death, just as one tries to have a good life. And if it's necessary to die fighting, then that's what we should do. If we're lucky, we can die peacefully. But few of us will ever live in such a world.

There always will be something worth fighting for and something worth fighting against. That's the drama of the human condition. That's what makes human life so interesting, and so entertaining, so full of laughs—the fighting, the struggling, the friction. I don't really want to live in a peaceful utopia. From a personal point of view, the world we live in is just fine with me. Because there are so many things to laugh at and laugh about, so many things to admire and to love, and so many things to despise. It's the ideal world for a writer, for anybody whose emotions are alive, for anybody who wants something to think about and talk about.

GARRETT HARDIN

In 1968, when the environmental movement was little more than a gleam in the eyes of a few enlightened ecologists, some sagacious friends of the Earth, and a handful of militant hippies, Dr. Garrett Hardin published "The Tragedy of the Commons." This essay is as provocative in its way as Thomas Malthus' "Essay on the Principle of Population" and has had a major effect on those who concern themselves with the fact of human overpopulation.

Dr. Hardin is currently Professor Emeritus of Human Ecology at the University of California at Santa Barbara. He has produced many books, including Nature and Man's Fate, Exploring New Ethics for Survival, Stalking the Wild Taboo, *and* Filters Against Folly.

Garrett Hardin is a true iconoclast who remains in the vanguard of environmental thinkers. His concepts are sometimes tough to swallow because frequently they attack precepts held sacred by many. Yet his conclusions are based on the thinking of a brilliant mind trained in biology augmented with a lion's share of common sense.

After meeting Garrett Hardin and having read some of his books and essays, I regard him as one of America's most

important critical thinkers, a man to be read and digested,
even if some of his notions get stuck in your craw.

———

JACK LOEFFLER   Dr. Hardin, would you reiterate the concept
that you developed in your paper entitled "The Tragedy of the
Commons?"

GARRETT HARDIN   Yes, it's a very simple idea, almost simple-
minded. I took as the example the historical instance of common pasture lands in England, which were called "commons,"
and pointed out that those worked very well, probably for hundreds of years. Then along toward the 17th and 18th centuries,
people became aware of the fact that something was wrong—that
the commons were being overgrazed and consequently they were
going downhill. The basic reason was that when people have
access to common lands on the basis of their need as they perceive it, and when the population grows to the point where the
number of people exceeds the carrying capacity of the land, or
the number of cows exceeds the carrying capacity of the pasture,
then each person, seeking his own self-interest, will put the
number of cows he wants to on the common pasture land. The
result is that presently there are too many, and the whole thing
is destroyed.

Now the reason this is a tragedy is because even after each
individual realizes what is happening, he is powerless to stop it,
because he says, "Well, if I don't get it, the pigs will." In other
words, my neighbors, who are pigs, will get it. So I'll take mine
before these pigs get theirs. Each neighbor reasons in the same
way. Although there's complete knowledge of what's happening,
the deterioration is inevitable. So this is like a Greek tragedy
where knowledge doesn't prevent the unfortunate end. Now, there
is an escape from this, of course, and that is to get rid of the
commons. Then you have two possibilities. Either you can turn
it into private property, as was done in England (unjustly, I may

say, the way it was done, but at least this will save the pasture land). Or you can turn it into public property, and then you have to appoint managers. And then you're at the mercy of the managers. If they manage well, it's fine; but if they don't, it isn't good. So there's no simple answer as to which one of the other systems will work better—private property (privatism) or socialism. Either one may work, or either one may not work. But the one clear thing is that the commons cannot possibly work once the population has become too great.

JL We're currently experiencing a true population explosion throughout the world. You recently published a wonderful paper entitled "An Ecolate View of the Human Predicament." I wonder if I may again ask you to reiterate the concepts that you developed within that paper?

GH This was simply an extension to a particular problem of the general idea I've just sketched. In other words, what I said there was that if we start talking about the global resources as if they are globally owned by everybody, and everybody should have access to them on the basis of their perceived need, then we will have created a global commons. My point being that we must not create a global commons, however well intentioned we are. Instead it is better to continue a system based on private property, which in this instance means national property—nations being the only large organizations that can enforce their laws—to continue to consider the globe as divided into numerous nations. Each nation has to take care of its own property. If it doesn't do a good job, it will suffer for it. Now that does not preclude trade between nations, but trade should be done according to the free market system. When you offer something for sale if you can't sell at that price, then you have to lower the price or you don't sell it. At any rate, there's a possibility of managing the global resources well, if it's done on a multinational basis, each nation managing its own property.

JL   You define lots of different notions with that. One of the notions that I was quite taken by was the whole sense of nature abhorring a maximum. Could you talk about the whole point of view?

GH   Well, that's a rather subtle idea, and I never realized the importance of it until a very unusual political scientist named William Ophuls pointed it out. This was his phrase, that "nature abhors a maximum." And what he meant by it was this: that if you settle on a single measure of excellence, such as profit in a profit and loss system, and decide you're going to maximize the profit, no matter what, you can be quite sure that before you get through you will have minimized some other value that you hadn't thought of, but which you really have high regard for. So the idea is, don't be so one-minded as to try to maximize any one thing. But instead, say here's a whole mixture of things I would like to have. Profit is one of them. Also, you would like to have beautiful scenery; you would like to have some wild animals, some wildlife, some wilderness areas and so on; and you cannot maximize all at once. What you have to do is to agree on some sort of a weighted system. How much do you want wilderness? How much do you want profits? How much do you want oil and gas out of the ground? You have to agree on limits for all of those and that's hard to do. That's a political problem, but you have to try. And if you can agree on how to weight these things, then you can develop a compound measure which it would be safe to maximize. Now that is very difficult; nevertheless, that's the way you have to go. Don't maximize a single variable. That's Ophuls' message.

JL   Concurrent with that, you developed the notion also of "shortages" and "longages." You have invented some terminology here, which I think is extremely important. If you wouldn't mind talking about that . . .

GH   Well, looking into the origin of the word "shortage," I discovered that it was invented about the middle of the 19th century, apparently in the Chicago grain markets—a perfectly natural thing to arise, where somebody said, "There's a shortage of this." A natural sort of invention. The interesting thing is that nobody ever invented the word "longage." To this day it doesn't exist, except in a few essays of my own, where I invented it. What's involved here, as I see it, is this: that the reason for the popularity of the word "shortage" is that when a person says there's a "shortage" of something, he means, "I'm going to try to get more of it." This appeals to his egotistical instincts. So everybody uses the word "shortage," meaning, "I want more." But if instead of saying, "There's a 'shortage' of supplies," one says "There's a 'longage' of demand," that ultimately boils down to the fact that there must a "longage" of people—too many people. And when you say that, then you have an argument on your hands. Because everybody says, "What, you mean me? How about yourself?" You see, you really fight against this idea of overpopulation. I think for the same reason that many people say there is no overpopulation, or there cannot be overpopulation, for that same reason we refrain from ever using the word "longage."

JL   Apropos of that, you attack the notion of foreign aid. Why do you think that providing foreign aid for so-called poverty-stricken people is a bad idea?

GH   First of all, I want to distinguish between two kinds of foreign aid—direct aid and developmental aid. Now, developmental aid does have a defense. This is aid in which you try to help other people produce more on their own. In other words, you give them a leg up, so to speak, but you don't permanently help them. You help them principally with information. Now that, there's a defense for. But I should say that it's very difficult to give good developmental aid. Nevertheless, in principal it can be done.

But direct aid, in which you come in when we say there's a crisis, a sudden shortage of food—this I think is very bad. This is the sort of thing that's happening now in central Africa and will continue to happen for many years to come. There are just too many people there. If you send food there, you keep the excess people alive, which means you increase the demand, because next year the population is increased, since you've kept everybody alive, including the breeders. The population in central Africa is increasing at two to three percent per year. So next year, things are worse; the demands are worse; these people will beat their environment to death at an even faster rate. So you're not doing them any good at all, even though you save lives. In the long run, you are ultimately causing the loss of more lives. Finally, the demand grows far beyond any possibility of helping it from the outside.

JL   One of the things that's interested me is your point of view regarding illegal immigration into the United States. How can we deal with something like illegal immigration?

GH   Well, there are a number of people in Washington, D.C., not government employees, usually, but some private organizations, who studied this for about ten years. On the basis of various trials, they're convinced that this can be handled. It's a question really of will to do it. Of course people who react adversely to it picture a Berlin Wall along the 2,000 mile border, and so forth and so on. This does not seem to be the central thing that's needed. We need to have security measures along the border, but they don't have to be perfect. The important thing is that there be no job for the person once he gets in, and that he know in advance there's no job for him. And that is soluble. The first thing we have to do is to get rid of the Texas Proviso.

In 1952, I think it was, the Texas Proviso to the immigration law specifically stated that the man who employed an illegal alien could not himself be regarded as violating any law. Well, you see, under those conditions he wants illegal aliens, because they're cheaper and they're not going to complain. This is just upside down. He is the one who should be prosecuted, rather than the illegal alien. Because the illegal alien's a poor devil. You can't blame him for trying to do something about his life.

And he's only one, individually. Whereas the employer may employ hundreds or even thousands. He's the big man, and he's the one who can do something about it. So if you make it a criminal matter, his employing the illegal aliens, then you're really putting pressure where it'll do some good.

Now, to do that, you have to have a system whereby he can reasonably be expected to recognize illegal aliens. What you do is turn it around the other way. Make it his duty to ask for the Social Security number of each person who is employed, which most employers do anyway. Then, having asked for it, he has to check that number with the office in Washington, D.C., to see whether it is right. If the guy whose name is Pedro Rodriguez gives him a number and he checks with Washington, D.C., and finds the number is registered to the name of John Smith, then the employer doesn't act as a policeman. Instead he says to Rodriguez, "Evidently, there's something wrong with your Social Security situation. Will you please go to the Social Security office and get it straightened out. And when you've got it straightened out, come back and I'll give you a job." Well, that's the end of it. That's all the employer has to do—verify this number.

We already have this sort of system in effect for credit cards. You present a credit card and they check either by phone or by wire, to determine that you haven't overdrawn your account. They do this instantly. This sort of thing can also be done for illegal aliens. We already have the system, we already have millions of people in the United States who are used to being asked for this sort of a card of identity. So the old objection to having an identity card, I think, no longer is as powerful as it was thirty years ago. We're used to it. So I think it could work. Once you've dried up jobs, then the word will get back into Mexico and Guatemala, and every place else, and people won't come in the large numbers. They say, "Yeah, you get in but you probably won't get a job, and you'll have to come back out poorer than when you went in."

JL   Do you see ongoing conflicts with the Latin American countries? In other words, do you foresee anything that could involve us in war?

GH   You know, I don't know how one can foresee. Think of the wars that have happened in the past thirty years. How many of them have I foreseen? Zero. There's conflict that's dangerous and we should take it seriously. My own feeling is, that if we keep our noses clean and tend to our own business, I don't think there'll be much danger. But if we think that we're the self-appointed guardians of some sort of political purity in other countries . . . well, our record in Korea and Vietnam is not such as to inspire confidence. I think we make things worse.

JL   But we seem to have a hallowed view of our own cultural point of view, which I think is the most dangerous thing we can do. I wanted to know if you had any thoughts with regard to our giving unwanted advice to other countries, along with our foreign aid.

GH   Well, as for the advice, I think every country should be free to give as much advice as it wants to, and contrariwise, free to ignore advice that it doesn't want. So, sure, we could give advice. But I think as far as foreign aid is concerned, say direct aid, I think very definitely we should set conditions. The principal one is some sort of population condition. In other words, if they show progress in controlling population, then we would be willing to give direct aid. But if they don't show any progress, it's just pouring sand down a rathole. We say, "We're sorry, this is useless. So we won't do it."

JL   It's difficult to approach a country regarding population control when their whole religious system tells them it's not correct.

GH   Well, I don't think the religion is very important in most parts of the world. I think we have a magnified view of this because of our own situation, where the Catholic Church, in particular, and then also the Mormon church, and a few others, do make this a religious matter. But this is exceptional. In most parts of the world it isn't religion. It's other influences. In some cases, it's just sheer supernationalism, where they are working with the old idea that cannon fodder and soldiers are useful, and you win wars with soldiers. Well, in a modern war you don't need cannon fodder, so that argument should disappear. But for many of the countries—well, they're fighting simpler wars, and maybe there's some justice in what they say, but we shouldn't support them in that. If they want to grow cannon fodder, let 'em grow it with their own food.

I think the basic reasons that produce overpopulation have been pointed out time after time. We had death control before we had acceptable population control. Now we've got acceptable birth control. It's accepted most places—take a place like India. The Indians have no religious compunctions, or any others, against using birth control. And they use it. But they use it only after they've had four children per family. Well, four children means doubling the number every generation, which is what India's doing. So you see, they don't have population control. The position of women is such in India that their value is chiefly in being mothers. They have the most power as mothers-in-law. That's the goal of every Indian woman, to become a mother-in-law. Then she's really sitting in the catbird seat. She can't become a mother-in-law until she's had sons, because it's the sons who bring in the wives that make her the mother-in-law in the family. And that's what she wants. So she's not going to stop until she has at least two sons, because one of them might die. If she has two sons, that means she's got, on the average, two daughters, and that's four children, and that's the trouble. How do you get into a value system like that and persuade them to live a different sort of life? That's something outsiders really can't do. They're going to have to do it themselves. How they're going to do it, god knows. Until they solve that problem, they won't solve the population problem.

JL   I know you've been a real torch-bearer for women's rights regarding abortion. Now that Reagan has been reelected, do you see any jeopardy to the Supreme Court law regarding abortion?

GH   That is a funny situation, because all the polls, ever since the middle '60s, have shown the majority of the people in the country are for abortion. The numbers and percentages have increased since the '60s. Politicians understand this, and mostly the members of Congress don't want to have anything to do with a move to change the abortion laws. On the other hand, the minority, the vocal minority of Catholics—not the majority of Catholics, but the vocal minority of Catholics—and the Catholic heirarchy put so much political pressure on the Congressmen that they don't want to be seen as standing up in favor of abortion. They just want to avoid it if they can. In this last session of Congress they finally changed the rules so that they avoided most of these issues. So in the last half of the last session, Congress was managing to protect itself against these unwanted amendments that were being tacked to everything that came along. You know, it didn't matter what the bill was, somebody tacked on an anti-abortion amendment. The battle will continue, but I think the worst is over. I think that the setting fire to clinics and blowing up clinics by the rabid "pro-lifers," as they call themselves, is likely to backfire and weaken the anti-abortion aspect. I hope so. At any rate, I'm not as worried now as I was, say, three or four years ago.

JL   One final thing I'd like to ask you to address, if you would—I think it was in 1972, the Club of Rome came out with their study at MIT. And in those days they were working with six major factors in predicting the probability of the human continuum continuing, so to speak. Could you update what you think the Club of Rome is about, and what their predictions are currently?

GH   Well, the Club of Rome prediction shouldn't be called that. It should be called a projection. The projection was that if we continue going in the same way that we have in the past, that presently we'll be in the soup. But this is a hypothetical projection and should be understood that way. It's not a projection of what will really happen. It's a warning rather than a projection. As a matter of fact, since 1972 we have mended our ways with respect to many things. Instead of the use of electricity going up eight percent per year, it went down for several years. And now it's going up at a much slower rate—two or three percent. You see, it is possible to mend our ways. We need people like the Club of Rome group to warn us to do so. Unfortunately, when they do so, and people do mend their ways, then along comes a body of people who say, "See, things weren't as bad as they said." Well, the reason they weren't was precisely because they said they were bad. So we need these Cassandras, but Cassandra never gets credit for what she does—either in Greek times or now.

JL   So you feel that there is hope for the human continuum.

GH   Well, I think we learn from sad experiences. If we're intelligent, we should learn a little bit ahead of the sad experience. In other words, we should recognize that when the miner's canary dies, maybe there's something wrong in the mine. We'd better get out before people start dying. If we'll only learn to recognize the miner's canaries in various situations, then we can avoid the worst disasters. But still, people don't learn from prosperity. People don't learn from success. That's one of the things that Kenneth Boulding says: "Nobody learns from success." We learn only from failure. The trouble with success is that we don't learn anything.

GODFREY REGGIO

When I first met Godfrey Reggio, he was known as Brother Godfrey and was a street-wise Catholic monk who has since doffed his habit in order to serve his fellow humans from his own expanded perspective. Over the years, my friend Godfrey and I have discussed many things, including the nature of the planetary environment and how captains of indusry are incurring capitalist punishment on Black Mesa, a landscape held sacred by both Hopi and Navajo and which coincidentally contains the largest coal deposit in Arizona.

Godfrey befriended the late Hopi elder and holy man David Monongye, who devoted much of his later life to trying to convince his people to remember their traditional ways and beseeching the white man to leave his land in peace. David fed Godfrey's inspiration, which was to become the classic film Koyaanisqatsi: Life Out of Balance, *regarded by many as one of the most important films of its time.*

Subsequently, the second film in the trilogy conceived by Reggio has been released. It is entitled Powaqqatsi: Life in Transformation, *and uses spectacular image and sound focusing on Third World peoples who are unavoidably affected by technofantasy. Currently, Reggio is working on the*

final film in the trilogy entitled Naqoyqatsi, *which comes
from the Hopi languages and means "War/Life."*

*Godfrey Reggio's great message to the world includes many
insights into the devastating effect perpetrated on our planet
by a culture committed to technology, extraction and
production for its own sake. His work brings to mind the old
Pawnee poem:*

> Let us see, is this real,
> Let us see, is this real,
> This life that I am living?
> O, you gods who dwell in all things,
> Let us see, is this real,
> This life that I am living?

GODFREY REGGIO   My background is not an academic background, though I attended a college. I think the little I do know
I learned from being involved with street gangs in the barrio of
Santa Fe, and then by extension in Mexico and New York and
Canada, and so the conclusions I've come to, at least the tentative conclusions, have been based initially on that experience.
The experience was one of seeing people who did not fit into a
consumer society; who did not fit into a monocultural society;
who had a cultural background which was basically being warred
against by the dominant culture. The experience became a source
of tremendous frustration and sadness when I went in, in a very
naive way, to make any substantial changes. The changes that
were made were more in the level of my consciousness than in
the level of being able to change, to work with street gangs. So I
feel that I was fortunate to learn it through experience, through
the knowledge of the heart, which to me can be a clearer line on
wisdom, perhaps, than the knowledge that the head gets through
programming and education.

JACK LOEFFLER   With regard to *Koyaanisqatsi*, your wonderful film which came out in 1982, could you describe the series of events that prefaced the actual production?

GR   I had set up with a group of friends, a collective, called the Institute for Regional Education. We had just come out of working in the Chicano movement in the Southwest, and nationalism became a very big factor. Not being Chicano, it was deemed best by all of us to form our own association based on a kind of mutual aid society. We decided to explore the impact of media as it relates to mass consciousness, which already gets into a severe contradiction—consciousness and mass consciousness and media. My own conclusions were that we live in a media world. All of our relationships are extended and we have given up our functional ability to have a direct relationship to the world. That being the case, living in a media society, not being able to wish that away, it became of interest to try to explore another use of media—not in an effort to make a reformation of the specific media form of television or radio or things of that nature, but to use it almost in a kamikaze sense. To use it as a vehicle of cultural organization.

So we developed a project through the Institute, with the American Civil Liberties Union, concerning the nature of police surveillance, behavioral modification, drugs to control behavior, such as Ritalin for children in school, and Prolixin, a death-inducing drug for people who are incarcerated, and the use of technology to control behavior. We did a nonverbal, nonnarrative campaign, buying TV spots and newspaper ads and radio spots at a saturation level for a month. In other words, what we did not do was pursue public interest advertising at the level that it's offered by the broadcast media, because that level is virtually without impact. We bought the time by raising money for a project and then had our TV spots in prime time, three times a night on each of the network affiliates, radio spots at drive time, when the traffic is highest, and billboards at high traffic dead city areas.

This allowed us to have an impact on people because of the nature of the society. We had written a book for the project, and we inserted it into the newspaper, as a Sunday insert. We felt that these kinds of messages were inescapable because of the nature of the society we lived in.

As a direct result of the project, legislation was initiated in the U.S. Congress to eliminate psycho-surgery (lobotomies) in all federal institutions. One of our representatives, perhaps doing the right thing for the wrong reason (the right thing being elim- inating psycho-surgery for poor whites and blacks who are insti- tutionalized), reacted because the polls reflected, as a result of our campaign, that people were interested in these issues. So a member of our congressional delegation was a cosponsor for the bill that ended up being successful in the U.S. Congress. I was quite excited that media could be used as a tool to help organize people around issues that related to their common interest, and I felt very elated by the success of the project. I was frankly sur- prised that more activists hadn't picked up on the same direc- tion that we had.

Subsequent to that I became involved in another film, a theat- rical film, that could offer people another view of the nature of the world they lived in—a world that would be characterized as dealing with mass density acceleration—a world that was no longer a society in terms of Northern Hemisphere industrial societies—a society that had lost its ability to take social con- cern as its pivot, and had moved to a system of living which was based on consumerism.

JL You're launching into a brand new project, which is a natu- ral outflow from *Koyaanisqatsi.*

GR The title is the North-South project—it's a theatrical fea- ture film, as yet untitled. When *Koyaanisqatsi* was being devel- oped, we saw it as the first of a trilogy. This film, the North-South Project, will be the second part of that trilogy. Essentially it will deal with the relationship between the Northern Hemisphere "over-developed" nations and the Southern Hemisphere "under-developed" nations. Our point of view is not against development per se, but raises questions about development with aid. When you develop with aid, you usually develop along a model that's prescribed by the dominant nation-states and the multinational corporations. That model is so pervasive at this point that a strong argument could be made for recognizing a global monoculture that's developing over the entire planet.

The film will try to show the difference between planetary consciousness and global consciousness. Planetary consciousness has a direct experiential base in terms of the place we live in, which I think the Southern Hemisphere has much to teach us about. Global consciousness is characterized by people who live in systems that no longer have a direct relationship with, or a direct experience of life, but who experience it through an intermediary called technology. Without making judgments or being didactic, the film will try to show a moment in the life of the planet through the power and intensity of the images that we see and the music that we create with Philip Glass and the composers of the Southern Hemisphere. We'll try to show, in terms of its simultaneity, the litany of life as it exists at any one moment on the planet during this part of the 20th century.

JL   Is it the wrong time to speak at all about the third part of the trilogy?

GR   It's not the wrong time, it's just that I wouldn't have much to say. It is a trilogy because I think three is a very important number in terms of a progression, and I felt that if the first piece worked well, it would be clear to me what the second piece would be. I would not have proceeded with the second piece if I did not feel clearly that the first piece, at least on some modest level, had an inspirational effect on people. Not an inspiration to an ideology or to an "ism" or a doctrine, but inspiration in terms of giving people a connection to their deeper selves, a connection beyond personality into something we might call "essence," which is not the easiest thing to get in touch with when life is surrounded by a consumer society. If we are so fortunate as to complete the second film, and it has some clear impact that is demonstrable by helping people connect on some conscious level with more knowledge, not information, about the world they live in, then I think the third piece will deal with an inner journey. That's how I'm seeing it right now.

I don't want to say I'd be making a film of the *Don Juan* books, but it'll be dealing with those subjects—personal alchemy, personal magic, the unlimited scope that a human being has, when the attempt is made to deal with the duality in which we exist in terms of the unity in which we all exist. So it would deal more with what you might call mystical or metaphysical subject matter, but in a very practical way, because these things aren't abstract. They exist in peoples' daily lives. That's merely a projection—it depends on what happens in the second film. The last movement in the second film will actually be an attempt to begin that process, which we hope would end in the third film.

JL You must have developed some interesting points of view through all of this, with regard to the nature of today's reality. Can you identify what you regard as two or three of the major problems confronting world culture?

GR It's a very difficult question, as I'm sure you understand. Rather than choose the stellar issues of overpopulation, nuclear war, famine and more conventional war that are clearly the major issues that confront all of us, I think it's important to step back and be realistic in terms of how we analyze the nature of what we see. These things—nuclear war, overpopulation, famine etc. —don't emanate from a vacuum. They emanate from a way of life. So to me the place to start is with an examination within each person's own consciousness, not necessarily through academics, or through think tanks, but through each person's own experience of life, with what it means to have a way of life.

Our way of life in Northern Hemisphere societies, industrial-technological societies, has by and large become so comprehensive and omni-present in its impact on people's lives on a daily basis, that I think we have lost our considerable ability to be reflective on the place we live in and the kind of life that we have. I think we've made enormous assumptions for the sake of our behavior, which is more than understandable. In fact one would almost have to have compassion for the situation that we find ourselves in, rather than blaming or complaining about it.

But I think our unquestioned way of life is akin to what in former centuries were religious beliefs, thereby putting us in the place that we're in. I further think that if you examine that way of life, you will find in it a bit of the Mary Shelley treatment of Frankenstein, not Hollywood's version, but Mary Shelley's version, which revealed the development of an autonomous being from a creation that man was involved in.

My own feeling is that society is no longer society. It's a system of living that has its own autonomous nature. That technique, which we enshrine as progress, is actually something that has its own life, like you have your life and I have my life. If that is the truth, then we have an autonomous technology that is at once something that we are totally dependent on, like we are dependent on air to breathe, or an addict is dependent on heroin for his continuance. We are dependent, without question, upon the mechanisms of technology to exist. If that mechanism is itself autonomous, or has its own being, its own nature, then we indeed have a situation that demands consciousness if we are to proceed in an enlightened way towards a new form of social structure.

So I would say that we should look beyond the obvious issues. I think the place to look most deeply is the nature of ordinary daily living. We require the pollution of the atmosphere, we require war, we require overpopulation, if we wish to maintain this unquestioned way of life, and it's that way of life that I think is being questioned by all these supposed horrors that are now rearing their heads.

The environment we live in is becoming, moment by moment, less productive of health, and joy of life. It's under a great deal of attack. It's at war. It's under siege by the world we live in. The same thing with war—war is a way of life now. We can't ask for world peace and continue to live the way we do. We have to deal rather courageously with cause and effect, with one thing motivating another.

On the other hand, who's to say what the future is to bring? I, myself, don't feel predictions are very useful because the little bit we do know is so small compared to the events and the forces that we're not conscious of because of our asleep state. Things that we interpret on the surface to be terrible might be the very things that cause the change needed to produce a more sane and balanced world.

We should not feel that what happens to the world depends only on us. I think the world might have many surprises for us. I think that technology, which is an artifice, has its own consciousness, its own beingness. I think that's true of the world in general. The Native Americans that I know have been very instructive to me in seeing the world as an entity of being, not in the scientific way or something without life to be used as raw material. If we believe in the world as a conscious being, it might be able to offer us some hope for the future.

JL   I know that you've been affected by the Native American peoples in the American Southwest. Do you feel that mythic man, or mythic peoples, have much to offer the technofantastically oriented people of the culture we inhabit?

GR   There's no question about that. I would want to back up. I think they have a lot to offer themselves, if they could believe it. The sad history of the Native American in the Southwest has been one of genocide and eradication of their way of life.

I think the best way for them to offer us something, which we clearly need, is to have them renew their own belief in their own traditions, in their own way of life, which is earth-rooted. We would have to see, literally, the breakdown of nations to be able to take the example of our Native American sisters and brothers. That doesn't seem so practical. What I'm saying is that I don't feel the mass society can be sane. I don't believe there's any liberal program, or revolutionary program, that can change the nature of the mass society. To get to a saner world, I think we need to break down the mass society, to decentralize our way of living. If we did that, I think we would find ourselves, in our own way, on some par of daily living with Native Americans. The communities of Native Americans that I know are fiercely anarchistic, and, in terms of their intentions, self-reliant. I'm not suggesting that we go back to the cave period, or to tipis. I think we could live in much smaller units. For example, the Bay Area could be the equivalent of a nation-state. That nation-state could have confederation to a union, but one without the power of a central government that determines all social, political, and economic life. I don't feel that this point of view is particularly impractical today because nothing else is working. I think we're at the point in history and time where that which was considered ideal is not mandated upon us as practical. I think it's a very exciting time to be here.

JL It would seem that there has been a lot of intervention perpetrated on so-called "third world" cultures by the so-called "civilized" culture of which we're members. I want to ask you if you have any notions with regard to how a culture may be left in peace to develop in its own fashion, a sort of cultural anarchism.

GR I think that day is over with. The whole planet is being impacted upon. Recently I was in some rather remote areas inside the Amazon basin, and I saw Indians who had lived undisturbed for literally thousands of years. Because of what's happening to the watershed and because of what's happening to the environment in which they live, they are being pulled out of their sockets. That's not an army that came in. It's the effect of progress and development, of Brazil wanting to open up the western part of their country to development.

So I think no living species upon the planet is exempt from impact upon its existence as a result of what's happening right now. I think that's part of the given, that's part of the mix. It can be deplored, or it can be applauded, depending on point of view. What is clear is that it's happening, so it's a given, it's a place to move from. It cannot be eradicated in terms of its presentness right now. So it can be the very thing that can bring about the changes.

We've had a period of maybe five to ten thousand years of "civilized" society controlling the apparent destiny of the planet. That period is coming to the end of a cycle, it appears. I'm not being apocalyptic or making predictions, but it seems apparent that the world is bent on destroying itself. That destruction might not mean the destruction of the world, but the destruction of civilization as we know it. That might be one of the most fantastic things that could happen. All of us would hope that it would not be accompanied by suffering, but the reality is, we're in a state of suffering, and that suffering is present with us right now. Do we want to suffer more? No, but it seems that that's the position we're in, that life has a determinism that's not human, that's not subject to human control, and that seems to be out of control. If it goes much further out of control, it could break apart. That breaking apart, that death, is perhaps the event that could bring about the life that the planet needs to continue in a more joyful way. I'm encouraged. I don't see the usefulness of trying to save the political, social, and economic structures, liberalizing them or humanizing them. I think they're basically unhumanizable.

There's a body of thought that could be characterized as futuristic. Herman Kahn was, until his death, one of the more quotable proponents of that. The Futurists feel that centralized high technology can be used to solve all of these problems and move us to a further progressive point. There are many who take issue with what. I stand with those.

ANDREW WEIL

In 1971 my wife Katherine and I were in the Sioux country of South Dakota talking to the Indian people about peyote and the Native American Church. One day, we had gone to Rosebud and were sitting in our truck staring at the front of the Bureau of Indian Affairs administrative office building. Everyone was out to lunch.

Parked beside us was a Land Rover inside of which sat a man who wore a most impressive beard. He was also intent on the BIA building. Finally we grinned at each other, got out of our vehicles and struck up a conversation.

"What are you up to?" I ask.

"On my way to South America," says he.

"How you gonna get there?" I ask.

"Gonna drive," says he.

"Very interesting," says I.

We introduced ourselves and proffered those thumbnail self-sketches whereby we justify our current presence on the planet. His name was Andrew Weil and he had just completed a book entitled The Natural Mind. *He was interested in the effects of psychotropic substances (as was I) and he was bent on finding true healers who inhabited cultures far beyond the reach of the American Medical Association. An interesting project for a man with an M.D. from Harvard!*

Andy Weil has published other books in subsequent years, including From Chocolate to Morphine, *which discusses addictive substances and was not well received in California. He is currently working on a book concerning home remedies and tending his own verdant and beautiful herb garden in the Sonoran Desert.*

JACK LOEFFLER   Well, Andy, you and I first met in October of 1971 up in the Rosebud Reservation in South Dakota. As I recall, you had your Land Rover all rarin' to go to South America. Could you describe the nature of the subsequent journey, and what it meant to you?

ANDREW WEIL   That was a long journey. You caught me as I was just at the beginning of the trip. I had been living in Virginia, and I'd finished writing *The Natural Mind* and was driving west in that Land Rover out to Oregon to see an old girlfriend and learn something about mushrooms. I stopped on the way to visit Leonard Crowdog, whom I had met a few months earlier, and had some very interesting experiences with out in Rosebud. I got to Oregon just at the peak of mushroom season.

That was really the beginning of my interest in mushrooms, and that's been ever since. In fact, at the moment, some of the major research that I do is on the subject of mushrooms. I'm currently putting together a project to investigate Oriental mushrooms, which are believed to stimulate the immune system, and have antiviral and anticancer effects, and which are virtually unknown in the West. No one has ever studied them medically. I then went from Oregon down to Mexico and spent several years in Latin America, mostly trying to visit shamans to learn about uses of hallucinogenic plants and psychoactive drugs in other cultures and other forms of medicine. At the end of all that traveling, I came back to the U.S., not really knowing what I wanted to do and not really fitting into the society back here. I had had a fellowship to do that work and one thing that I found was that when I got back and the fellowship ended, I didn't easily fit into any kind of job market up here. You know, I'd been away for three and a half years. I had been doing weird things down in South America, and I couldn't seem to find any niche up here. I also found that I couldn't really stop traveling. For a number of years I bounced around the country, mostly between Oregon and Arizona, and finally settled in southern Arizona. I had seen so many things, and had so many experiences, that I needed some time just to sit back and distill out of that what I got.

One of the things that I found was that a lot of what I was interested in while looking around South America was really up here. For example, I had been very interested in trying to find miraculous healers of one sort or another. I saw a lot of healers and I saw a lot of shamans. The best healer that I have come across since then turned out to be in Tucson—an old osteopath, who's now eighty, who uses only manipulation, and quite regularly in this little office down on Grant Road produces what I think are miracle cures. And he has a very interesting theory to explain it. That just seemed to me to be very symbolic in a way. You know, they tell that you don't have to go further than your own backyard, but I suppose sometimes you have to go away to learn that.

I saw a lot of interesting things to do with plants and the way that native peoples use plants, and that's always been another of my interests. I work now with an organization that I helped found called the Beneficial Plant Research Association, which is headquartered in Sausalito, California. Our purpose is to try to educate people to the wisdom and value of using natural products in many areas, in cosmetics and pharmaceuticals, in food. I think a lot of our health problems in this culture, as well as economic problems really stem from not using plants correctly.

47

And that's just a matter of not understanding. I think that is something that I learned in those travels down there—to be around traditional peoples who use plants in careful ways, without changing their chemistry or isolating elements from them, and I think seeing that made a great impression on me. I'd like to try to introduce that up here as much as possible.

JL   A subject that really interests me concerns traditional people, whom I've begun to think of at this particular time as mythic people who are still motivated by some mythic process within their own culture. Do you have any thoughts with regard to the role of mythic man at a time when we're technofanticized almost into oblivion?

AW   Well, one thought that I have is that this is the age in which mythic man is going to disappear. I was very aware of that in going to remote areas in Latin America, and some in Africa. You always want to see the unspoiled culture, but you're part of the spoiling of it. That's a strange paradox. But this is the age, the first time in history, that primitive cultures will disappear. I think that must have enormous symbolic significance. One thought that I have is that what you call "mythic peoples" really represent the childhood of the human race, that this is the end of that phase; and while we may regret that loss greatly, that's what's happening. It seems to me that, ideally, we shouldn't lose that, that what's best about those cultures should survive and be part of the adult phase of the human race. Maybe we're about to grow up, finally.

JL   One of the things that I've wondered about, and am still puddling around in my own mind about, is some means of preserving genetically, or in any fashion, what those folks have to teach us, which we seem to have forgotten. There are processes that may have atrophied in us.

AW   Well, my hunch is that nothing has really been lost—that it's really in the realm of collective consciousness, that it survives. We haven't really lost that or become disconnected from it; it's just that it's been overlain by other ways of using the mind and using consciousness which keep us out of touch with that way of perceiving. I think that the potential is there for us to connect with those roots in our consciousness, and as I say, to perpetuate what is good about those traditional cultures. The other idea that I have is that while it's very easy to romanticize and idealize those cultures, they have fatal flaws in them, as evidenced by the fact that when they meet us they get put out of business. I think there is an inevitability to that progression, and because we're in the time in history when those cultures will disappear, it's our chance now to discover and adapt to our own mode of living what's best about them.

JL   With regard to that, how do you foresee your own role in future events, using what you've learned?

AW   Well, I still don't quite know where I fit into things. You know, I'm a physician. I don't really believe in a great deal of what I was taught in medical school. I would very much like to see change come about in medicine, because I think that plays a key role in our society. Here's another analogy with your mythic peoples. Physicians today really have replaced the roles of priests and shamans in traditional cultures. If you lived in a mythic society and there was an eclipse or the crops failed, you'd go to the priest to find out what happened and what to do. In our culture, we go to doctors. All of our hopes and fears are rationalized in medical terms, in terms of medical dangers to health. That's what we do with drugs, that's what we do with eclipses, even—we tell people not to look at them because they'll go blind. Because medicine has that role, I think it could be a key in bringing about large-scale change in society. If medicine could change its philosophical orientation, I think that would free up a lot of other things that are now stuck in this culture, get things moving. I think I have some part to play in that—I'm not quite sure what it is. It feels very frustrating at times, because modern medicine is such a monolithic structure. And to my mind its way of thinking is so off the mark at the moment, particularly in its ignorance of and blindness to the reality of the nonmaterial and the power that plays in shaping the material world. If that could change, I think it would be a very key change, and I would like to play some role in bringing it about.

JL   I recently read some of Edward Wilson's stuff on sociobiology, and Wilson is totally convinced, as far as I can tell, that everything is genetics; and I can see, to a certain extent, where he's coming from. But is there more to it than that?

AW   Well, here's an interesting little anecdotal piece of evidence that I think bears on that. I've recently been interested in all of the attention that's been given to cases of multiple personality disorder. Now, this used to be an extremely rare condition, and many psychiatrists doubted its existence. They thought it was an artifact of the interaction with the therapist. Suddenly, it's very in. There are lots of cases of it, and for the first time, it's getting lots of research attention. There was recently the First International Congress on Multiple Personality Disorder. One of the aspects of multiple personalities that has not been mentioned much, which to me is the most fascinating, is physiological differences between the personalities that can be measured. For example, there was one case where there were twenty-some personalities, all but one of whom were right handed. Now, handedness is supposed to be genetic. There have been cases where one personality had a violent food allergy. If that personality ate this food, and another personality took over within a certain period of time, the allergy wouldn't appear. The feeling you get reading this stuff is that the brain is infinitely programmable: that the genetic code provides the hardware, but the software can be changed. A lot of the phenotype of the human being, including, I think, behavior and many disease processes is software; I don't think it's hardware. Even with the same genetic blueprint in place, there can be radically different expressions. So that's my perspective on Wilson. I think he's right from his limited perspective, but I think there's a larger perspective in which that's one aspect.

JL   I'd like to ask you about your writing. You've written several publications, now. Your first was *The Natural Mind*.

AW   Right. Then I wrote a book called *The Marriage of the Sun and Moon*, which was a collection of articles that I'd written during that period of traveling. Then I wrote with coauthor Winnie Rosen a book called *Chocolate to Morphine*. It's about all the psychoactive drugs in our life, truly from chocolate to morphine. The idea put forward is that there are really no good or bad drugs; there are just good or bad uses of drugs. And there are a lot of people today who don't want to hear that. There are a lot of people who would like to believe there are bad, nasty drugs that we should make go away. And the people who get so exorcised about that really fail to look at the obvious drugs in our midst that we don't even call drugs, the most obvious of which is tobacco. That really is the most addictive drug known— far more addictive than heroin. It's the only one that regularly exposes nonusers to the drug. We're paying for it with our tax dollars, you know. There's just great irrationality there. A lot of people don't like to be shown their irrationalities, so *Chocolate to Morphine* has been very controversial. There are still fights going on, mostly in California, as to whether it should be banned from libraries and schools and so forth.

Early this year I published a book called *Health and Healing*. I'm very glad to have that out so that I have something out about something other than drugs. *Health and Healing* is about the nature of medicine and treatment and a review of a lot of different systems of alternative medicine, which is my current interest. It's really the first half of a longer work. I'm now working on the second half of that, which is more specifically about medical self-care. I very much believe that the responsibility for health is the patient's, and that there are simple ways of learning to take care of yourself that can reduce your disease risks and minimize the chance that you need major medical intervention. And I'd like to try to give people an idea of that.

I really feel that the kind of medicine I do is preventive medicine. That's what I'd like to be doing. I don't mean preventive medicine in the formal sense. There's a speciality called preventive medicine, but it has to do with immunizations and sewage systems and that's not what I'm interested in. I'm really interested in how to teach people not to get sick. Mostly I would like to work with well people. I'm a little frustrated right now that the people who come to see me as patients are not only ill, but by and large, desperately ill. I don't know quite what to do to attract people who are well, and consult with them to try to identify the factors in their lives that are likely to cause trouble down the road that they can now change. It seems to me that that should be the main function of physicians—to dispense that kind of information, so that we don't have to have the kinds of expenditures of money and time and energy and suffering that we now do to deal with illnesses once they've reached the stage where your options are very few.

JL   So, basically, you're initiating the idea that preventive care is the best route to take.

AW   No question about that. That's an obvious idea and it's annoying to see how little of the medical curriculum is now devoted to that. Take the case of cancer, which is, I think, a good example to look at, because treatments for cancer are, to put it politely, unsatisfactory. That goes for alternative treatments, as well as regular treatments. That's not a disease that we can deal with very well. There are a few forms of cancer, like leukemia that we can treat fairly well, but most forms of cancer we can't treat. You know the medical establishment now says that at least ninety percent of all cancer is environmentally related. That's a big reversal in thinking from when I was in medical school. If ninety percent of cancer is environmentally related, then ninety percent of cancer should be preventable. And if we're not preventing it, why aren't we? I think there's very specific, simple information that you can give people to reduce the cancer risks in their lives. But you look at the teaching that goes on in medical schools today, and except for talking about lung cancer being due to smoking, all the information that's given is geared toward the diagnosis and treatment of cancer once it appears. There's no information given about how to prevent cancer. And certainly not how to explain to people what cancer is and how to reduce their cancer risks.

JL   Do you think that attitudes have much to do with getting cancer?

AW   I certainly think they're a factor. Cancer looks to me like a disorder of the immune system. The immune system is failing to do one of its jobs, which is to recognize and weed out malignant cells as they occur, which they probably do all the time. There are a lot of environmental and internal pressures on cells to turn malignant. But most of those malignant cells never get a chance to develop and give rise to a tumor, because the immune system recognizes them and weeds them out. So it looks as if the development of clinical cancer has to do with failure of immunity. Recently, a lot of research is coming out that shows the connections of the mind and nervous system to the immune system. There's a whole new field now, called psycho-neural immunology, about that. And once you show that there are ways that stress and mental attitudes can influence your body's defenses, then you have a whole lot of mechanisms to explain how stress can make people susceptible to infections, or how over a long period of time, certain kinds of mental attitudes might favor the development of cancer. I don't think that's the be-all and end-all of it, but that's certainly one important factor.

JL   That brings something to mind. A friend of mine recently had an unusual malady, and he quit using marijuana because he had discovered some sort of evidence that indicated that perhaps marijuana attacks the immune system.

AW   Well, that idea has been put forward in the literature, mostly by people who are very antimarijuana. The evidence for it had to do with test tube studies and certain observations that I don't feel were very well controlled. The epidemiological evidence from cultures where marijuana is heavily used does not support the idea that there are any kind of significant changes in susceptibility to infection or immune disorders in a marijuana using and non-using population. That doesn't mean that for a specific person there might not be an effect. It also doesn't mean that if a person believes that marijuana is a factor in harming his health, and that if he gives it up, he might not feel better, or have better health. This could be due to his belief, rather than anything the marijuana was doing to him. At the moment, I think the only proven health hazards of marijuana use have to do with respiratory irritation from smoking. I think otherwise, it looks like a relatively mild drug compared to things like alcohol and tobacco, in terms of what it does to health. And I don't think there's any good evidence that there is any significant effect on human function.

JL   Do you ever work closely with herbalists?

AW   I do. I don't swallow everything that I hear from herbalists. I am interested in finding medicinal plants that have reliable, reproducible effects. You know, I'm all for chamomile for relaxation. But I'm also interested in things that are stronger, that have real medical effects and can be used in place of synthetic drugs. The problem with the information from herbalists is that it's quite varied in its quality. You'll find one plant and a hundred indications for its use. Or you look up one particular kind of condition, and you find a hundred plants that have been mentioned for its cure. That kind of nonspecific information is not very helpful to doctors. I'm interested in trying to get more doctors to use more medicines in natural form. For doctors to do that, I think they really have to have a sense of the chemistry and pharmacology of a plant and a sense that it's got regular, reliable, reproducible effects from person to person. So, in my own investigations of herbal medicine, I find that a relatively small percentage of the plants that I come across, that are advertised to me or described to me in books by herbalists, really hold up when you give them that way. But some certainly do, and those are the ones that I'm the most interested in studying.

JL Is there an existing pharmacopoeia of natural medicines that you feel is comprehensive?

AW No. I think there's a real need for that. One of the projects that I have thought of working on at some point is a real compilation of the Chinese herbal pharmacopoeia, which is vast, and I think not really understood well in the West. That would be one thing I'd like to see. And I think something that was analagous to the *Physician's Desk Reference* for herbal preparations would be very useful. But there's a long way to go before we have that. There's just an awful lot of information to sort through to try to verify and see whether these things are real or not. The problem is, a lot of the statements about herbal medicine, I think, have been passed along from person to person. Sometimes I think some of it is just crystallized superstition, and there's really no experimental evidence to back it up. So it'd be nice to sort out the real reliable drugs, like cincona bark, which quinine comes from, and willow bark, from which aspirin is derived, from the ones that mostly function as placebos. Not that there's anything wrong with placebos. I'm all for them. But it's useful to know which plants have a real pharmacological basis for their effects, and which have relatively little.

JL Has the world of ethnobotany yielded much, or is there still a long way to go?

AW There is a long way to go. One of the problems has been that there has been very little financial support for ethnobotanical work in recent years. When I first was in that field, when I was in college in the early '60s, we were just at the end of a cycle in which corporate America was very interested in ethnobotany.

That followed discoveries in the '50s of plants like Indian snakeroot, which gave us reserpine, and the discovery of the vinca alkaloids, which are used in the treatment of leukemia. Somewhere around the mid-'60s that period ended. And since then it has been very difficult to interest pharmaceutical companies or other corporations in natural products. I sense that right about now that's beginning to change again.

You know, I think these things wax and wane, but it definitely seems to me that corporate America—this time for truly economic reasons—is suddenly realizing that there's a market out there for natural products. So I've begun to have inquiries from a number of corporations that I have never heard from in the past wanting information about plants as new sources for ingredients in products. We're living at a time when supermarkets have natural food sections, and that's a major change in America. That's in a lot of odd places. I spent last summer in a very tiny town in northern Idaho, and there was a Safeway nearby that had a very extensive natural foods section. That to me is a major change. I think that because of the realization of the economic value of natural products, corporate America is again willing to look at ethnobotanic investigations. So we'll see what that produces.

JL I know that you're really interested in going to the Orient. What interests do you have over there, and what do you think you might find?

AW Well, in October of '83 I was coleader of a mushroom tour through China. And this was the first Chinese-American mushroom exchange that had taken place. In October of this year, I was on similar travels in Japan. Mushrooms have been very good to me. They have taken me lots of places. My interest in Asia, at least the parts that I have been, is again in plants, and in traditional uses of natural products. Japan and China are probably the areas of the world where there is most use of mushrooms, both as food and medicine. And that's tremendously interesting to me. I have a great desire to spend some time in Southeast

Asia. I was there a long time ago, in Cambodia and Thailand. I'd really like to spend some time in Indonesia and Sri Lanka and Malaysia. I'm particularly interested in trance phenomena over there, and music and dancing, and, again, in some of the traditional foods and plants that are used both as foods and medicines and for other purposes. So I am less interested at the moment in spending time in Latin America. I've done a lot of that—there are parts of it that I'd like to see that I haven't, but at the moment I seem to be more oriented toward Asia than I was previously.

JL When you say music and dancing, do you think of it from the point of view as a physician, or an enjoyer of music and dance?

AW No, it's more than just an enjoyer, although I'm interested in it as a technique of consciousness alteration and of mind-body development as well. And I am interested to see what of it I can incorporate into my own life. I very much like that kind of thing.

JOHN NICHOLS

NORTHERN NEW MEXICO *is an empty land of amazing light*
that plays against the mountains, the plains, the clouds, the
sky. Humans have passed across this landscape through
millennia out of mind. Currently, at least three distinct
linguistic phyla are represented by the Puebloans, the Navajos
and Apaches, and the descendants of Europeans.

Located near the base of the western aspect of the Sangre
de Cristo Mountains is the town of Taos, wherein lives a meld
of Puebloan, Hispanic and Anglo people who have struggled
to achieve a state of relatively peaceful coexistence. Since the
turn of the present century, Taos has become home to an
array of independent thinkers comprised of artists, writers,
filmmakers and happeners (people who either cause things to
happen or to whom things happen).

Currently, a fine American writer, John Nichols, lives on
the edge of town where he can watch the play of light on the
mountains and in the plain. He is the author of many
provocative novels and collections of essays. His New Mexican
trilogy includes The Milagro Beanfield War, The Magic Journey
and The Nirvana Blues. *John's highly evolved sense of his*
home ecosystem is reflected in his works of nonfiction,

including The Last Beautiful Days of Autumn, If Mountains Die, On the Mesa, *and* A Fragile Beauty.

John is an avowed Marxist who bears a deep sense of social justice and injustice. He lives as he believes, simply and frugally, in his old adobe house beside the acequia *that nurtures the land with water. He is a grouse hunter, a fly fisherman, a real participant in life, a good friend.*

———

JOHN NICHOLS   It seems like you can't do art right without being conscious of just trying to keep culture surviving. It's almost like everyone is forced into that position because they're all standing on the precipice, watching things that they hold precious getting rubbed out. I'm working on this book called *On the Mesa*; I've been working on it for a couple of years. It started out that I wanted to write a book that was a combination of beautiful, naturalist lyrical writing about land that then connected with a kind of doomsday ecology, which is very prevalent, from Rachel Carson and Ed Abbey to Barry Commoner to you name it. Then I wanted to push it one step further into radical politics, which is where a lot of people stop. They don't get into the real implications. I've long felt that most ecologists get a lot of information and it adds up to worldwide ecological problems. But then they stop short of saying what you really do about it. People like Abbey are just wonderful writers and essentially could have an extraordinary amount of power, I think. But it occasionally gets subverted by a kind of anarchist's point of attack where they talk about what's wrong, yet they shy away from then trying to develop the power to really change it, really articulating what it is about society that makes it wrong. My feeling has always been that the first place you look is in the functioning of capitalism today in America. It seems as if many of our best ecologists and conservationists stop short of that. Because the minute you start talking about that, people start screaming, "Pinko, crypto, commie, socialist, no-good-for-nothin' radical!" Yet to me it's always seemed that when you have an economic system whose major tenets are planned obsolesence and conspicuous consumption, which is American climax capitalism's major litany, you basically are dealing with an economic system that's run on a formula for planetary suicide. People are really afraid to say that, because it means essentially overthrowing the system that we've got, in order to change the systems in the United States and Western Europe. We're six percent of the world's population, yet we consume fifty percent of its resources every year. If you want to get into the next twenty-five percent of the world's resources, they're probably consumed in Western European nations and Japan, which doesn't leave much to the Soviet Union and Third World countries. Four-fifths of the world's people do not really contribute to the destruction of the planet. People stop short of really talking about that.

What I was going to do, to make a long story short, was to try and write a book that was lyrical, that was ecological doomsday, and also have beautiful, naturalistic photographs. Ansel Adams, Edward Weston, Elliot Porter. Then throw in some real radical politics, pushing the sort of conclusions of most conservationists and ecologists much further than they've been pushed.

I basically look at the world from a Marxist perspective. Which doesn't mean to say that in the Marxist world . . . however, I think that all humanity is going to have to redefine materialism because there's as much danger of socialist countries also destroying the planet as there is of capitalist countries doing it. It's just that capitalist countries are light-years ahead. We carry the weight right now, therefore we carry the major responsibility.

So I tried to do this book and I just never could get the rhythm. I couldn't merge all three things. I'd get this beautiful lyrical writing going great, and it's no problem then to switch and start quoting facts about the destruction of the planet from local examples on up to treatises on the greenhouse effect and evidence of just how little time we have left. But then I would sit down and get into my political rap, which would just always come down real angry and real polemical and real soap-boxy. I couldn't figure out how to merge everything in that beautiful, seamless manner that combines beauty and outrage in the articulate way I wanted to. I keep rewriting the book, and I keep taking photographs. One of the ways that photographs really help me is it's an excuse to get out. It forces you to walk through the landscape, really paying attention. It heightens your awareness, which is wonderful for me. I also figured it would be a way of really disarming a lot of people, to have beautiful and serene pictures—and then I could slip in the knife.

JACK LOEFER   How can you slip in the knife?

JN   Well, that's real difficult. There's a real resistance. It's kind of strange, because even the major critics of how we're destroying everything have trouble making that link. People keep talking about using the capitalist system to correct the ills that the system creates. And I just think that's a real conflict. It can't be done. The system gives lip-service to finding solutions. But basically there's a conflict within a system that depends on waste, depends on conspicuous consumption, depends on planned obsolesence for survival, depends on a 5.5 percent growth rate every year. Abbey had a wonderful quote in one of his books about how our economic system must expand or expire. I think he coined the phrase that "growth for the sake of growth is the ideology of the cancer cell." And nothing could be truer. But people don't say that what you have to do is radically change. Without some kind of enormous social and economic change, it's just going to go on.

JL   I've been coping with the same problem for a long, long time. The question that I've got is how do you change it? How do you turn the juggernaut around or disarm it?

JN The most important thing you do, I guess, is education. People really aren't going to turn a juggernaut around unless they can make the connections and understand how those connections work. Most people don't connect. For example, I'm sitting here burning wood in this wood stove. As long as I'm burning wood, everyone in this area looks at that as being ecologically sound. You're not strip mining Black Mesa for bituminous coal. I don't even cut down green trees. I just pick up slash and old dead stuff, so I'm not contributing to the destruction of forests in that way. Except that burning wood is like burning a fossil fuel, and it's a major pollution contributor. It's as destructive as burning natural gas or burning butane, or burning anything like that. And so ultimately what I'm going to have to do is get into solar energy or something like that—because the economic philosophy behind everything else is real destructive. It's important when you begin to realize that. One of the things you're going to have to train people in this country to accept is a radically altered standard of living. You know, I sort of make a point of living real cheap. My energy consumption bills every month are just real low. I live in a sort of shitcan house. I use an outhouse. Even though I just have a little piece of land, I irrigate those fields and take care of them and let my neighbors take the produce, because just having that produce in the economic chain is real important. They've all got a few cows and chickens and goats and they can use it. Training people to feel those responsibilities on even small levels is real important. Population is an extraordinary problem in the world. But the biggest population problem exists in the United States. That is the most serious population problem on earth, because every time a North American child is born, that child is going to put a demand on the earth's resources that, in its lifetime, would take 5,000 Bolivians to meet, or 10,000 Bangaladeshis to meet. You understand? So the most serious threat to the physical survival of the planet is when a North American child is born. Therefore, the most immediate necessity for population control, if you're concerned about the survival of Spaceship Earth, is to really curtail any kind of population spread in Western Europe and the United States. It's not a billion Chinese that threaten it, or 800 million Indian people who threaten it. There are reasons that that kind of population really destroys the functioning of a third world country, but it's not the third world countries that put the demands on the planet's resources that threaten its survival, that threaten with the greenhouse effect, that threaten the destruction of all our fresh water supplies with acid rain. That's coming from America and Western Europe.

There's a book by Arthur Koestler called *A Ghost in the Machine*. I have not read it, but my father did, and talked to me about it, and used it in lectures in class. Apparently the major argument in that book is that as our brain has developed and filled up this cranium, and got bigger and bigger and bigger in proportion to our size, we have actually mutated the genetic instinct for survival—that it has been crippled. It no longer exists. We have developed to the extent that we no longer have that instinct built into our system genetically. One of the major canons of the capitalist system is to get everybody believing that. The concept of Doomsday is a very important one in our culture. You know that ultimately it's screwed, it's out of control, we can't save it. Therefore everyone should eat, drink and be merry because tomorrow we die. Not only that, but that kind of attitude forges a kind of cynical mindset that makes the system run perfectly, a kind of competitive system where everybody's out for everybody else, *sauve qui peut*. The virtue of selfishness becomes one of the tenets of our society. We justify the exploitation of other people—survival of the fittest. Darwinian natural selection becomes another major ball bearing upon which the capitalist system turns. And we all believe this intimately, so that we don't function as a community. We can't save it, so let's just exploit it as long as we can. And that's a major doctrine that keeps our system functioning. So the struggle is to educate people out of that, because it's phoney baloney. Because it's wrong.

JL   But how can you do that?

JN   You do it in little bits and pieces, by every person who writes a book, or Ansel Adams taking a photograph, or you doing a radio show and trying to get people to articulate ideas. You do it at every level that you can, every way that you can, I happen to put a lot of overt polemics into my art. One of my struggles is to learn how to juxtapose and meld polemics and art. But I also feel we live in an increasingly nihilistic society. So anybody who does anything to counteract that—to make positive contributions that fly in the face of and defy that kind of gloom and doomsday thing that keeps it running—is being a politician. I often tell people even if all you do is paint pictures of sunflowers in some kind of positive and joyous way, that's a real political act, because you're doing it in the face of a society that rewards you much more for nihilistic, exploitative, emotionally deficient, culturally vapid, fascist entertainment. Just insisting on having a little plot and growing your own healthy vegetables is a political act against a country whose basic food growth and distribution system is fascist—in that increasingly the food you eat is devoid of nutrients and coated with chemicals. Which means you're eating food to nourish yourself that is actually an important link in the cancer chain that's going to kill you. So if you just grow your own kind of food, that's a real political act. Learn a little bit about organic gardening and try and spread it to other friends. Turn 'em on to what a tomato really tastes like. That's a beginning, right?

An important thing is then to try to teach and train people, try to reeducate people out of the way they've been brainwashed. That's essentially what I do in a lot of my books. It's why I will agree to almost any interview, because inevitably we're going to discuss this shit and you'll put some of it on the radio. So it's worth a day, or whatever, to do it. Because that's another little glitch. And also we'll have a conversation and I'll learn something, and you'll learn something, and we'll turn each other on. Those are the connections. The fact is, one of the major things is to teach people, to train people to see the connections.

ALVIN JOSEPHY

ALVIN JOSEPHY IS ONE of America's most distinguished American Indian historians. For many years he was editor-in-chief of American Heritage Magazine. *Alvin attended Harvard University, was a Marine Corps sergeant in the South Pacific during World War II and has been the president of the National Council of the Institute of the American West. He is the author of many books, including* The Patriot Chiefs, The Nez Pierce Indians and the Opening of the Northwest, The Indian Heritage of America, *and* Now That the Buffalo's Gone.

Alvin and I met at a meeting of the Center for Arts of Indian America in Gallup, New Mexico, in 1968 and have remained good friends ever since. During the early 1970s we worked together to try and save Black Mesa in the heart of Hopi and Navajo country from being strip-mined to provide coal for power plants at Page, Arizona, and Bullhead City, Nevada.

Over the course of our friendship, we have frequently discussed the importance of the values of traditional peoples whose points of view are molded by both their cultural mythic structures and the evidence of their five senses. We both regard these traditional points of view as vital to

*the collective human species and rue the twilight that
threatens to enshroud traditional man and his sacred sense
of the land.*

———

JACK LOEFFLER   In your most recent book, *Now That the Buffalo's Gone,* you actually delve into the histories of several different groups of people. and one of the things that's very interesting
to me, and probably little known to many people, is just how
long some of these groups of people had actually been here prior
to the coming of the Europeans, and that our continent actually was fraught with historic heritage, whether it was written
history in the sense that we know it, or was transmitted as oral
tradition. Could you talk a little bit about the cultures that
existed on this continent prior to our own?

ALVIN JOSEPHY: Well, to me that is a very interesting aspect of
the study of American Indians, or peoples of the Western Hemisphere. A lot of it, of course, we still don't know, and some of it
is still very controversial. People have different ideas about it.
But because it is speculative to a large degree, and is based on
discoveries that are being made all the time, it's like a detective
story. We're still going at it. When did men first come over here?
Who were they? How did they come? I think it's pretty well
accepted, since no remains have been found in the New World
of pre-*Homo sapiens* man, that man did not develop here. He
evolved elsewhere in the world, and came over, undoubtedly
across from Siberia. When that happened is still open to question. It now looks pretty much as if man first began to come,
if he hadn't already come, around thirty-five or forty thousand
years ago. Just at that time, Neanderthal man still existed in
Eurasia. And Cro-Magnon man, the successor of the Neanderthal
man, also existed. He was coming into more and more promi-
nence, but Neanderthal man was still on Earth. Now, that was
a very early period, a very old period. There's no evidence that

Neanderthal man got here. In fact, Cro-Magnon man was more developed; he had learned how to make a higher stage of tools and weapons. He was more advanced technologically than Neanderthal man. That's, perhaps, one of the reasons why he persisted and Neanderthal man died out.

With his more advanced abilities and knowledge, he was able to expand, to migrate into areas where no man was known to have been before, into the less hospitable parts of the world—the colder regions. He got up into Siberia and was able to venture across what was then the so-called Bering land bridge when it appeared. And Cro-Magnon man, *Homo sapiens sapiens*, got across into the New World.

Now, who those people were, we don't quite know. They came from Asia somewhere, probably in small groups. They began their expansion over the two Americas. A lot of them must have eventually reached South America and been the oldest ancestors of the American Indians in the Western Hemisphere. Later groups arriving after them took on more and more of the physical attributes of the later developments of man's physical features. For instance, the more Mongoloid an American Indian looks, the later his ancestors got over here, because that was a later development among men in eastern Asia.

If some of these groups came that early, man has been here a heck of a long time. They evolved while they were here. They merged with later groups. They maybe fought with later groups, fought and split apart, and there were various meldings. All kinds of scientific fields must be brought into play to try to sort it all out, particularly linguistics. That field has shown that maybe there were 2500 mutually unintelligible Indian languages in the New World at the time of Columbus, but they all seem to go back to a certain limited number of superstock languages that came over from Asia at different times—possibly as few as two, three or four. The study of that will show the migrations of these people. It will show their mergings with other peoples and the development of new languages as people split apart or melded culturally and invented new words for new things. But you're perfectly right in saying that we ought to look with awe on these people who came over from Asia, let's say thirty-five thousand years ago, bearing their values and beliefs and understandings. Once arrived in this New World they began to adapt over those thirty-five thousand years to new ideas, new understandings, new values. They borrowed from others who were there with them, or whom they met, and adapted in an evolutionary way to their environment. They created not only cultures of their own but value systems and relationships between themselves and their supernatural worlds. None of this had any relationship to what was going on in Europe. It was long before anything began to go on in Europe.

Man's relationship with nature, developing here independently of the way it developed in Europe, first of all brought about clashes when the Whites came over here. It's continued to a great extent because, as the White man has spread out over this whole continent and exploited everything in sight, it has brought about the kind of clash that can mean finality for the other point of view, for the Indian point of view. That finality has not occurred yet. There are still many pockets in the Indian world, here on certain reservations, among certain groups of Indians—not the whole tribes in many cases, but parts of tribes—where Indians have been steadfastly opposing that type of development and exploitation of what's left of their land and resources. It so happens that the non-Indian environmental movement has found a commonality of interest with those Indians trying to do the same thing on the last unexploited parts of the lands from which the Indians have been dispossessed and are now owned by the Whites themselves. However, it's a question today whether things have gone too far and whether Indians or Indians in coalition with Whites can prevail against the opposition. And if so, for how long. Because as long as the Indians change materially, there is this conflict between their desire for material profits and their value systems. They are under great pressure to sustain themselves. The question is whether a nation, like the Navajos, are going to be able to maintain enough control over their resources to be able to protect those resources the way the traditionalists want them to be protected. Or will they assert control and play the White man's game with it, and brush aside their traditionalists?

That's where we are today, it seems to me. I don't know who's ahead. So far the traditionalists have managed to exert influence probably beyond their numbers, and certainly beyond their political strength. But they've had certain things helping them, including the legal decisions. Whether those decisions eventually will be overturned, brushed aside, I don't know.

JL Those people are largely sustained by their own mythic process, it seems to me.

AJ But the point is, how long will that go on? There are certain numbers of them who are sustained, but can they continue to hold that line, hold the fort, in other words. They're holding on with fingers that are getting whiter and whiter to the bone.

JL That's true, and the industrial complex is moving in with greater rapacity. It seems to me as though integrity is only on the side of the traditional people; that there's a remarkable lack of integrity from the developers.

AJ Well, what you're almost saying is that the traditionalists are not capitalists. I think eventually we're going to have to bite the bullet and say that capitalism is a big culprit here. Capitalism is the driving force and the profit motive is the driver. There are too many people who don't want to say that. They don't want to face that reality. They're afraid of being called Communists or Socialists or something, because what is the alternative? When you say that capitalism is the culprit, the alternative must be that, "Well, you're a Communist; you want to overthrow the capitalist system." But philosophically, politically and economically, if you say that capitalism drives people to exploit, it's the traditionalist who stands in the way to fight it, because he is not being motivated by the same forces. The traditionalist is not, per se, a capitalist who is going to make his living by the profit motive.

JL   Would you think that the monotheistic situation that we have culturally is a flaw from the point of view of our approach to the natural environment?

AJ   Well, the word "flaw" is the word you fall over. It depends whose perspective you're looking at this from. For an environmentalist, it's part of the problem. If Indians look on themselves as part of their universe—that they are attached spiritually to the spirits of everything in creation around them, not just the birds and the animals, but rocks and natural forces like thunder and wind and lightning—everything, animate and inanimate, and they are no higher or lower than that, and they must stay in balance with all of those other forces of creation in order to maintain harmony and well-being within themselves and their group, why that's a totally different relationship of man to nature and man to the supernatural than the Christian or the Jew or the Muslim, all of whom view their relationship to the supernatural in an entirely different way.

JL   There's a school of thought proposed by certain people like Paul Shepard, that indicates that when man stopped being a hunter-gatherer and became an agriculturist he missed the boat; he got caught in some strange force that was to result ultimately in disaster. I'm not sure that that's true, but it's interesting historically to see what's happened when we've broken from the traditional point of view where we're related to all things to where suddenly we transcend all things. It's possible that the gene pool will remain intact as long as the Earth remains intact; but what about the attitudes necessary for human survival on the planet today? Do you think that man can survive under the predominant set of attitudes that have been perpetrated by our culture, or do you think that man needs to assume, or reassume, some of the attitudes that prevailed among so-called traditional peoples? AJ Well, I think that is happening; and if it's happening, it's happening because man has discovered the need for it. For example, I've just talked about the spiritual attachment that the American Indians have with the spirits of everything else in creation. Some people call it paganism or heathenism; others would call it animism; it's certainly non-Christian. But that circle of interdependence which maintains harmony and balance is suddenly discovered to be not so dissimilar from the ecological circle in which everything is related. You break one rung of the ecological circle and everything goes awry. Everything in that circle becomes disoriented, loses balance, loses harmony. That, in a way, is the circle of the environmentalists today. They see the interrelationship, which they didn't see years ago. They're striving to maintain ecological harmony as well as they can, so it's a new discovery for the White man, or the European-based person. And yet, it's exactly what the Indian has been doing in the past.

But I was going to ask the question, can a traditionalist become a capitalist? Now, I have seen, for instance, on the Fort Peck Reservation of Montana, Sioux medicine men who are on the boards of directors of capitalist industries run by the tribe up there. These men say, "I can be both, I'm both. I preside over the Sun Dance and then I put on my business suit and go and sit in a office in A & S Industries," which is the biggest industry in the state of Montana. It's on the Fort Peck Reservation; it's owned one hundred percent by the Assiniboin and Sioux tribes of that reservation. They have contracts with IBM and other industries, turning out all kinds of products—huge stamp presses—it's a big operation, tremendous. They do have contracts with non-Indian organizations to help them in certain ways, but the last time I saw it, it was fabulously successful. It showed how people who continue with their traditional ways also fit into a capitalist structure. That is something that Indians will be facing more and more. There's all kinds of pressure now on the reservations to turn away from dependence on the Federal Government and get into the world of private industry—get into joint venture operations and make contracts with the exploiters and the people who want to develop their reservations. Keep reservation government all-Indian, let reservation government maintain a certain amount of control and management over their resources; but get money from private industry rather than the government. That means going into profit-making ventures, so that there'll be profit coming in which they may have to split with Whites, or even get from Whites. But that will sustain their government and their people, and raise the economy of the reservations, and do all the rest of the things that the Federal Government has failed to do or has made worse.

Now, what happens to the traditionalists and traditional beliefs and values when that happens? This is a whole field of inquiry all by itself, just as you might say, "What happens to an Indian kid who is brought up in a traditional way and feels he understands and lives by the values and beliefs of his people and his ancestors; he goes to school and then goes away to college, gets a Ph.D. and becomes a professor of English, or a writer, and lives in the White man's world?" This is a question that's being faced by a lot of Indians today. "Am I no longer really an Indian? How important to me are my values?" Well, he may strive to keep them important and may really achieve that, but he's then got to have his kid adopt the same understanding and beliefs. But the kid may have lived off the reservation all his life, lived in an apartment or a private home, and really know nothing about Indian life. So the question is not, "Will Indians vanish," but, "Will Indianness vanish?"

ANNA SOFAER

THAT THE WESTERN HEMISPHERE has been inhabited for many millennia by fellow humans is not contested. However, many of us who belong to the monoculture of mainstream America have an absurd tendency to overlook, or worse, to deny that the inhabitants of the New World prior to the advent of the Spanish conquest were capable of major intellectual achievements. Only recently, for example, have scholars begun to comprehend the scope of ancient Mayan culture whose denizens independently invented the concept of zero!

In an arid region in what is currently considered northwestern New Mexico is the canyon called Chaco where the ancient Anasazi people architected spectacular buildings whose ruins have piqued the interest of everyone who has ever stood in their shadow. In 1977, Anna Sofaer, an artist from Washington, D.C., visited Chaco Canyon. She was interested in petroglyphs and carried in her mind the recollection of a recent seminar concerning archaeo-astronomy. She climbed 440-foot-high Fajada Butte to look at a spiral petroglyph that had been pecked into the southern face of the top of the butte. It was lunchtime on a day in late spring and Anna Sofaer and her companion sat in the shade near the petroglyph to relax and eat. As she watched, a dagger of sunlight passed near the center of the spiral. In a flash of intuition, Anna recognized the site as an Anasazi solstice marker.

It is an astonishing intellectual feat that a group of the Anasazi, ancestors of today's Puebloans, were able to calculate the time of the solstices using the noonday sun and a petroglyph enshadowed by great slabs of rock. It was also a moment of inspired intelligence when, a thousand years later, Anna Sofaer was able to extrapolate the significance of the ephemeral dagger of light.

After a decade of intense research, Anna has studied both the characteristics of the land around Chaco Canyon and the accompanying Anasazi ruins. She has discovered that the structures were almost perfectly oriented to the passage of the sun and the moon. Her tentative hypothesis is "that the Chacoans oriented, proportioned and located their buildings in a pattern focused on the sun and the moon into the ceremonial center of their regional culture, Chaco Canyon."

Since her discovery, Anna Sofaer has produced a documentary film entitled The Sundagger *and has written numerous articles which have appeared in scientific journals.*

———

JACK LOEFFLER   Anna, I'd like to ask you to describe your first encounter with the Sun Dagger on Fajada Butte.

ANNA SOFAER   In 1977 I went into Chaco Canyon. I had already become involved in Mayan astronomy and had a strong interest in prehistoric astronomy and rock art. I finally decided after years of work in my studio that it was time to get out and actually see some of the rock art I had only looked at in books. I subscribed to a newsletter called "La Pintora," which was the American Rock Art Research Association's newsletter. It told about a group of volunteers who were going to Chaco for a couple of weeks in June of '77, and that they needed people. I just signed up. I had no idea what Chaco Canyon was. I had never been in the desert, or really to the Southwest. It was on that trip that the director of the group, Jim Bain, a retired colonel from Albuquerque who had organized the whole thing, said, "Well, nobody's ever recorded the rock art on Fajada Butte."

A fellow from California who was an excellent climber and seemed to be well-equipped and ready to go, needed somebody to accompany him. Everybody else was a little scared of the snakes and the height, and were savvy about what to be afraid of. I was so naive I just went along. He seemed to know what he was doing.

The first day we went up and recorded about twenty sites. We decided to go to the top out of curiosity, and see what else might be there for the next day. We got there kind of late in the day and saw a spiral, a large spiral, about fifteen inches across, behind the rock slabs. But it was late, so we decided to come back the next day and record it. When we came back, we happened to get there at about noon, about a week from summer solstice. And the dagger of light was right through the center of the spiral— very, very close to the center. It was so vivid that at that moment I said, "It's recording the highest point of the sun in the day and the year, being close to noon and summer solstice. My partner said, "Mmmmm. . . . whatever you say!" But I felt certain from the imagery of it.

Three weeks earlier, in my craze for rock art, I had gone to a conference of the American Rock Art Research Association, where they showed endless slides, which I loved, of rock art. One fellow showed that remarkable site in Baja, California, where a shaman figure with horns is painted on the wall of the cave. As he found out, at winter solstice sunrise, light comes through the cave and a horizontal dart crosses the eyes of the shaman just at that time of year, marking winter solstice sunrise. That image came to mind as I saw the Sun Dagger on Fajada, and helped me understand what it was. Plus the fact that three months earlier I'd had the opportunity to be in Yucatan, and to see the great pyramid of Chichen Itza. At equinox as the sun sets, the shadow form gives shape to the great serpent that's carved at the base—so you get the head of it carved in stone, and going up the carved steps to the top of the pyramid is the light shape of the rest of the serpent. It's absolutely marvelous, as the sun sets at equinox, casting the shadow from the edge of the pyramid to make that rippling shape of the snake. So those two experiences plus a little bit of study of Mayan astronomy, and having been at other sites which use shadow and light, gave me some assurance.

I didn't have any previous knowledge of the Chaco culture, of Southwest Indian culture. But there was a linkage; the shadow and light spirals had some connection to earth-sky imagery. I'd just finished a work of art of my own, which dealt with the same imagery. It was called "Stone Serpent in the Sky." It developed a lot out of the imagery of the Mayan astronomy I had studied in Washington. I had tried to bring together an almost ambiguous quality of earth and stone and sky, so that the shape was sculptural and also galaxy-like. When you think about it, the spiral with the dagger of light and the connection of the sky and earth there was so similar.

JL   Can you describe the site on top of Fajada Butte?

AS   Yes. It's three large rock slabs that are six to nine feet in height; they lean against the cliff face in a nearly vertical position so that the openings between them, which are oriented to the south sky, channel light in on the cliff face behind the rocks. That light comes in as vertical forms. There are two spirals carved on the cliff face behind the rocks. About midday, every day, light will come in in vertical forms on the spirals, but in a very particular form at summer solstice, equinox and winter solstice. At summer solstice, a light dagger bisects the larger spiral right through the center, coming down in a vertical shape. Then at winter solstice, that light dagger has moved far to the right and a second light dagger has joined it, so that they bracket the large spiral, holding the center empty of light at the lowest time of the sun—winter solstice. At equinox that second light dagger, pierces the center of the little spiral. So you have the three points in the solar cycle marked with the same kind of imagery each time.

JL What's your theory with regard to how this all came about?

AS Somewhere between 900 and 1300 A.D.—and possibly we can pin it down to around 1000-1150, when the Chaco culture was in its fluorescence, and building solar-aligned, elaborate architecture—the Pueblo people carved the spirals. That is, they pecked them out on the cliff face. They shaped the surfaces of the rocks that cast the shadows that formed the light patterns, and may also have adjusted the rocks to some extent to make the particular forms they needed. The site is really quite complex in the number of light patterns.

We've found in the last three or four years, in addition to the light daggers at midday, that as the sun or the moon rises, there is a separate set of shadows on the same spirals. Not only on the same spirals, but in the same key positions. So the center, where the light dagger comes at summer solstice noon, is crossed by a shadow at the minor standstill position of the moon. And the left edge of the same spiral is marked with a shadow for the major standstill position of the moon. Each of these shadows is aligned with a diagonal groove pecked by the Anasazi, probably to emphasize them as markings. We've written in detail about the solar and lunar markings in science articles and presented them at conferences of archaeoastronomy.

So, the site marks five separate solar and lunar positions in a set of six markings, that repeatedly use three key points—the center and two outer edges of the large spiral—which really define the spiral's size and shape. There's no way to know with certainty whether the rock slabs were moved and shaped, but it seems likely that it would have been easier for the Anasazi to do it with some adjustment to the slabs' shapes and their positions.

JL   Have you extrapolated any reason for all of this from the point of view of the ancient Chacoans?

AS   Well, yes, now that we have noted more markings and we know more about the orientations of the pueblos. We've read a lot of the ethnography and talked to Indian people. First of all, there are seven other markings on Fajada Butte, using five other petroglyphs, just the way the Sun Dagger does. These are spiral forms, often crossed with dagger shapes of light, and a rattlesnake, aligned with the shadow edge. These markings give the time of solar noon—that's when the sun passes across the meridian—in distinctive configurations for each season. So you have a separate marking for summer solstice noon, winter solstice noon and equinox noon. And not just one marking—but multiple markings for each of these times. For instance, at equinox noon, at a site on the east side of the butte, the snake and a spiral are simultaneously crossed by shadow, while at a west side site, a spiral and rectangular form are marked with a dagger of light going through the center of a spiral. This pattern of multiple markings, so often in pairs, clearly seems intentional. We have now recorded a total of thirteen markings on the butte, several of which involve meridian passage, which is solar noon. Now we are looking in the canyon and analyzing, as others have already, Pueblo Bonito, probably the most central and important of all the structures of the Chaco system, which extends through the San Juan Basin, 30,000 square miles. Many of the archaeologists feel that Pueblo Bonito may be the very center of that system. Certainly the canyon is, and Pueblo Bonito is the most important pueblo in the canyon. Perhaps the roads are coming right to Bonito and joining at its great kiva. When you survey the orientations of major walls in that pueblo, you find that the east-west wall is within a quarter of a degree of east-west; and the north-south wall that divides the pueblo is within a quarter of a degree north-south. Now the reason that ties into the Fajada markings, and begins to show a kind of pattern of cosmology and the use of the same astronomical concepts, is that to know noon to within a minute, you need to know north-south within a quarter of a degree. There's an equivalent accuracy; and the same is true for east-west and equinox. If you know the day of equinox, which seems to be true from the markings on Fajada Butte, you know east-west within a quarter of a degree, as is shown in Pueblo Bonito. But it isn't only the equivalent accuracy. These alignments in Bonito are, in a sense, a spatial expression that correspond to the temporal expression of the light markings. For instance, the mid-wall could be seen as the axis of the day the way the solar markings of noon are axes of the day. The east-west wall could be seen as the divider of the year, just the way equinox is the midpoint of the year. The joining of those cardinal alignments at the most sacred, central place in the culture is, I think, kind of a complementary structuring of space and time on the canyon floor, equivalent to the markings on Fajada Butte, which is that vertical axis drawing in the sky markings from above.

JL So these are people who were totally oriented to the sun?

AS The sun and the moon and the cardinal directions, and finding themselves in time and space by marking the center points and the extremes of the astronomical cycles. The solstices are the extremes; the equinoxes are the mid-point in the solar cycle; and the moon's two standstill positions are its extremes. All of these points have been marked on Fajada. There's yet another shadow as the sun and moon rise that comes at zero declination, the midpoint of their cycle, to the far right edge of the large spiral. And again, the seasonal markings join together the sun's annual daily cycles. It's a constant bringing together of these complementary positions. It's so integrated.

JL   How would they have used this information?

AS   Well, I suppose in the beginning my colleagues thought of it as a device or an instrument. I resisted that a bit, but I think not enough. More and more, it seems to me, and the Pueblo people with whom I've spoken, including the Hopi people have expressed this feeling—that it's a sacred site—the Sun Dagger and the other ones as well. The butte itself is sacred. What was happening there was in a ceremonial context, of commemoration of these important times. There's such a redundancy in the markings. They're so remote. They have such vivid imagery—degrees of light through spirals are not just instruments or devices or calendars. They're really, I suppose, cosmic symbols for finding one's place in the center of time and space.

We've had the chance now to look throughout the San Juan Basin. With Mike Marshall, an archaeologist very knowledgeable about the Basin, I have now climbed or done an aerial survey of all of the prominent geological forms—anything like Fajada Butte. We've done about twenty of these surveys, and found only low-walled structures that appear to be shrine-like sites. But we've found almost no rock art, and nothing of explicit astronomy. So it's as though the butte were the unique center in the Chaco culture for that kind of ritual astronomy. Recently the director of the Chaco Research Center, the archaeology study center of the Chaco culture, has come out with his conclusion, after many years of study, that Chaco was not really lived in consistently. It was visited periodically, in what he called "ritual pilgrimages" to the canyon. One wonders if the ritual activity that centered in Chaco wasn't timed or linked in some way with those markings on Fajada. Hopi people have told me that one or two people might watch something like the dagger of light at that site, and that those people would have the responsibility to then tell the people in the canyon when to begin the ceremonies.

86

The complexity of the astronomical information is so striking—and so important to grapple with, to understand. And the accuracy, for naked-eye astronomy, is astounding too. But I think more than just the complexity and accuracy is the aesthetic context—the beautiful quality of putting all that on what in some cultures might be like a pyramid, or massive temple. It is a beautiful natural structure, Fajada Butte.

TRAGEDY IN INDIAN COUNTRY

WHEN I FIRST PASSED through Hopi and Navajo country in the late 1950s, I was truly overwhelmed by the physical beauty of the land, the great sense of space, and the sparseness of the human population. The march of the electric kachinas bearing power power lines from electrical generating stations to the urban centers of the West had as yet to mar the mythic landscape. John Wesley Powell had as yet to have his name immortalized by a lake whose presence I hope he would have detested.

Several years later, in the early 1960s, I lived for some months in a traditional forked-stick Navajo hogan near the base of Navajo Mountain, Utah. I spent part of every day with traditional Navajos, few of whom spoke English. I speak no Navajo. Little by little, I came to realize how distant my headset was from these people for whom the very landforms had mythic meaning. It gradually became apparent to me just how presumptuous my culture had been by imposing religious and secular mores on a people whose culture was already rich and meaningful.

In 1968, I was at Shonto near Black Mesa, which is a landmass sacred to both the Hopi and Navajo. The Hopis live on the southern three promontories of Black Mesa and the Navajos lived in isolated family groups in hogans scattered over the top of Black

Four Corners Power Plant, Hopi Indian

89

Mesa north of the Hopi land. Big Mountain lies near the heart of Black Mesa. I heard rumors about a coal mine that was going to be developed. In 1968 I had no idea that Black Mesa contains an enormous amount of coal, which is, incidentally, the only significant coal deposit in the state of Arizona.

In 1970, my good friend Bill Brown, who was then the historian for the Southwestern region of the National Park Service, informed me that a huge strip mine was scheduled for Black Mesa to supply coal for two electrical generating stations. The first power plant was to be located close to Page, Arizona, near the shores of Lake Powell (or Lake Foul, according to Ed Abbey). The coal was to be transported by train across the incredibly beautiful and fragile Kaibito Plateau south of Navajo Mountain. The second power plant was to be located at Bullhead City, Nevada, and the particles of ground coal were to be slurried in water through a pipeline. The water was to be pumped at the rate of two thousand gallons a minute from an ancient aquifer that lies beneath the arid surface of Black Mesa—an aquifer that feeds the springs which serve the Hopi villages to the south. The generating stations would belch bilious billows of smoke into the pristine air of the Four Corners, where the states of New Mexico, Arizona, Utah and Colorado meet. The surface of Black Mesa would be razed relentlessly. Indeed, in 1972, I was present when the hogan of an elderly Navajo woman was bulldozed into the ground. The woman's world of a lifetime disappeared before her weeping eyes in a cloud of dust, and then she was homeless.

Bill Brown wrote an essay entitled "The Rape of Black Mesa." A small group of us founded the Black Mesa Defense Fund, the purpose of which was to rally traditional Hopi and Navajo peoples in defense of their own land, to provide logistical support for them, and to inform the people of America of this greatest of cultural and environmental tragedies, perpetrated in behalf of growth and economic development for its own sake.

Following World War II, government and private industry grad-ually coalesced into a united front against which the traditional Indian people resisted heroically. But the cards were stacked against them. Their tribal councils were manipulated by their hired Anglo attorneys, who reaped lucre while they went about their business in blatant conflict of interest. Norman Littell rep-resented the Navajos and John Boyden represented the Hopis. (Ironically, the tribal councils themselves rarely represent the will of their respective peoples.)

The *Healing vs. Jones* decision of 1962 (so named after the chairmen of Hopi and Navajo Tribal Councils) determined that Navajo and Hopi Indians had joint and equal rights to the reser-vation established in 1882 outside the boundary of District 6, which remains exclusively Hopi country. This Joint Use Area was not slated to be partitioned until twelve years later after intense lobbying by several Arizona congressmen including Sam Steiger.

The traditional Hopis and Navajos formed an alliance that was attacked by the Congress of the United States when it proposed that the Joint Use Area be divided, specifying which land was Hopi and which was Navajo. This was to result in the reloca-tion of as many as ten thousand Navajos from their traditional homeland. This concept received Sam Steiger's fiat. (Steiger, inci-dentally, once called me the arch enemy of the environmental movement as I was about to testify before a congressional com-mittee on which he sat. If there was ever a case of the pot call-ing the kettle black . . . !)

The Joint Use Area (JUA) comprises much of the Big Moun-tain area of Black Mesa. The JUA, as such, has a history which began in 1882, when President Chester A. Arthur issued an exec-utive order allocating 2.5 million acres around the Hopi mesas for use by the Hopis and "such other Indians as the Secretary of the Interior may see fit to settle thereon." The Hopis and the Navajos suffered some boundary disputes, but on the whole lived side by side in relatively peaceful coexistence, at least since the time when the Navajos returned on the infamous "Long Walk" back from the edge of extinction in the 1860s.

The history of Indian land and the U.S. government is long and sordid, the government constantly jockeying for position within the context of jurisprudence to ultimately get at Indian land or its contents. The government assumes a false appearance of integrity within the patina of "doing what is best for the Indians." There are several publications that deal with the "rape of Black Mesa" and relocation of the Navajos. None fully encompasses the entire composite of factors within factors. The Central Arizona Project lies at the heart of it. The mission at the CAP is to pump three million or so acre-feet of water out of the lower Colorado River into central and southern Arizona, ostensibly for agriculture but realistically to provide developers and growth-mongers what they need—water to convert the beautiful Sonoran Desert into a human wasteland for the sole purpose of making lots of money.

At the time of writing, the Peabody Coal Company of East St. Louis continues to strip-mine Black Mesa, edging ever closer to land scheduled to be vacated by its Navajo inhabitants. To date, some six thousand Navajo souls have been forced to move from their homeland. No one really knows where they have gone. They have disappeared into the border communities of Tuba City, Gallup, Flagstaff, Winslow and elsewhere, but no more will they tread softly on the soil of the land they know as home. The Navajos who remain are those stubborn, pesky redskins who show no fear of the U.S. government and its lackeys. These are Navajos whose relationship to their land is stronger than the will of the prevailing bureaucracy. These people are an embarrassment to a power structure that itself will finally come to be regarded as wrong and possibly even evil.

In the three sections which follow, aspects of the Black Mesa/Big Mountain debacle are described by a group of Hopi elders, a group of traditional Navajos, and a former U.S. Secretary of the Interior.

A TRADITIONAL HOPI PERSPECTIVE

On the afternoon of March 16, 1971, I was invited into the kiva at Hotevilla, Arizona, to record with pen and paper the points of view of traditional Hopis regarding the strip mining of Black Mesa by the Peabody Coal Company of East St. Louis. This interview is a composite of the opinions expressed by several Hopi elders, and is extracted from an essay published in Myths and Technofantasies, *a publication of the Black Mesa Defense Fund.*

————

A blind man, one of the oldest of the Hopi elders, stood atop the kiva and shouted that there was to be a meeting. I followed as he descended into the ceremonial chamber, a large subterranean room lighted only by the sun's rays passing through a small opening in the roof. He built a fire with cedar wood in an old stove at the center of the kiva, and went to a receptacle containing several ceremonial pipes. He took one of the pipes and filled it with Indian tobacco from a leather pouch. He quietly smoked the pipe, and with each puff he sent his prayers to his deity.

One by one, several Hopi men from Hotevilla and neighboring Oraibi drifted into the kiva. For a while they spoke to one another in the mellifluous Hopi tongue. Small blue corn tamales were

Hopi Prophecy Rock, Third Mesa

roasting on top of the stove. After the tamales were cooked, they were put into a basket and placed in the center of the room for all to share.

Finally a Hopi man, fluent in English, rose and said: "It is very difficult to translate Hopi into English because the Hopi language is very different from English. You can say things in Hopi that no words can say in English. This is because the Hopis think differently than the whites. Anyway, I will try to tell you what is being said."

"What you call Mother Nature is everything important to the Hopis. It is the land, the water, the trees, the rocks, the animals— all living things. It is everything. It is the force or the power that comes from these things that keeps the world together.

"We sit here in the kiva which is the womb in the Earth. This kiva is our church and our school. Here in the kiva is where our leaders work. It is where we have our ceremonials, here in the Earth, so that Nature will work in harmony with people. When we have ceremonials; this keeps the natural forces together.

"A long time ago, many generations before the white men came, the Great Spirit came to this place. He was the first one to come here. The Hopis asked permission from him to come and live here. The Great Spirit told the Hopis that they could live here, as long as they lived according to his teaching. The Hopis agreed to do that.

"The Great Spirit told the Hopis that this place here is the spiritual center of this land. This is the most sacred place, right here in this mesa. This is where the Hopis must pray for all things on this continent, because this is the spiritual center. The Hopis pray for balance so that all things will be well and healthy. The Hopis remember today what the Great Spirit first told them long ago. The leaders pass it down and teach the young people what the Great Spirit first taught the Hopis. This is better than writing it down, because this way we all know what the Great Spirit first told us.

"Before the white men came, all the Hopis were happy and sang all the time. Every morning, the people got up at dawn and ran to the springs to bathe in the cold water. This makes our hearts strong. After breakfast, the people would run to the gardens to work all day long. Some people have gardens in Moenkopi, fifty miles away. In those days, before the white men came, they ran all the way to Moenkopi and worked in their gardens. After working all day in their gardens, they ran all the way home. After dinner, the people would weave or have ceremonials. All the time they were running, or working, they were singing. They were singing all the time. Everyone was happy in those days.

"The Hopis didn't have any class structure at all—no bosses, no judges, no policemen—everyone was equal. No one had more than he needed. There weren't any politics then. Everyone lived together in harmony. We had ceremonials so that everything would stay in balance with Nature. In those days, the air was clear and everyone could see far. We always looked to the Earth Mother for food and nourishment, and we never took more than we needed. Our lives were very rich and humble. We lived close to the Earth as instructed by the Great Spirit.

"When the white men came, everything started to get out of balance. The white brother has no spiritual knowledge, only technical knowledge. He made the white man's government which tries to take away the Indians' land. For a long time the government did not try to take away our land because they didn't want it. The land here is very dry and barren, and only the Indians know how to live on this land. The Great Spirit taught us how to live on this land.

"Then in 1935 or so, the Bureau of Indian Affairs (BIA) convinced a few people to have a Hopi Tribal Council. Almost no one wanted it—only a few people who had been educated in the BIA's schools and had learned the white men's ways. All of the people on the Tribal Council were Christians, either Mormons or Mennonites, and they had forgotten the Hopi religion. Now the BIA has made schools here and they make our children go to these schools. The children don't learn the Hopi way. It takes a lifetime to learn the Hopi way.

"Then the Hopi Tribal Council signed a contract with the Peabody Coal Company to come up here to Black Mesa and take away the coal. The Hopi people didn't even know about the contract for a long time. Clarence Hamilton was the Chairman of the Hopi Tribal Council. The Council did this for money. This was illegal. And then the Peabody Coal Company was already on Black Mesa.

"Now there is a big strip mine where coal comes out of the Earth to send electricity to the big cities. This makes upheaval on the land. They cut across our sacred shrines and destroy our prayers to the six directions. We send our prayers in all directions so that there will be balance. We are not to use the Earth in a way that is destructive.

"Peabody is tearing up the land and destroying the sacred mountain. What they take away from our land is being turned into power to create even more evil things. They use these things in war. The Hopis don't believe in wars. "Hopi" means "peace." The BIA educates our children in the white men's ways and then the government makes them go off to war. We don't want this for our children. It turns them into 'Kahopis.' 'Kahopi' means 'bad Hopi.'

"Peabody is taking water away from this land. We pray that the rains will come so that we will have good crops. It is very bad that Peabody takes away the water, because it upsets the balance of things. You can't do things like that and have Nature be in balance. The white men do not understand this. When they burn the coal, it fills the sky with poisonous gases. This will hurt the people and the growing things. The Hopis know that you can't treat Nature the way Peabody is, or something will happen.

"The Hopi prophecies are drawn on a rock on Black Mesa. The prophecy says that there will come a time of much destruction. This is the time. The prophecy says that there will be paths in the sky; the paths are airplanes. There will be cobwebs in the air; these are the power lines. Great ashes will be dumped on cities, and there will be terrible destruction; these are the atom bombs that America dropped on Hiroshima and Nagasaki. The prophecy says that men will travel to the moon and stars and this will cause disruption, and then the time of the great purification will be very near. The Great Spirit says in the prophecy that Man will not go any further when he builds a city in the sky. People are planning to build a space station. When that happens, it will be the time of the great purification.

"We Hopis have been here for many years. We have our own religion that teaches us how to live in harmony with Nature and with each other. The white men have tried to make us into Christians. The Christians believe in manmade things, but have forgotten about natural things. And so everything is out of balance and is falling apart. If the white men would stop trying to teach us Christianity and would begin to listen to what the Great Spirit taught the Hopis, then everything could get back in harmony with Nature. As it is, the white men are destroying the Earth. You know about Jerusalem. It is a sacred place of the Christians. They would be very angry if someone went in and started tearing up Jerusalem."

MONSTER IN DINETAH

THE FOLLOWING IS A transcription of a radio program that I produced in 1982. It concerns a land dispute between the Navajo and Hopi Indians of Northern Arizona. The dispute is largely an invention of the United States Government and private corporations. One outcome would result in the relocation of up to 10,000 Navajo Indians from their traditional homeland, thereby making that land available for the extraction of natural resources.

The following text is selected from recorded interviews with eight Navajo women and one Navajo man, most of whom live in the Joint Use Area at Big Mountain, Arizona. Each new voice is indicated by a space.

———

A monster has come into the land of the Dineh. [*Dineh* is the name by which the Navajo people know themselves. *Dinetah* is their name for their homeland.] This monster is attacking the minds and spirits of the Dineh. This monster is tearing up the heart of the female Black Mountain in order to feed itself so that it can continue to grow and eat and grow and eat. For over 100 years the government in Washington has been pushing this monster deep into Dinetah.

Powerlines near Shiprock, New Mexico

In 1864 the Belagonnas [white persons] came and rounded up the Dineh and herded them like cattle to Fort Sumner. In 1868 the Dineh made the long walk back to the land of our ancestors. We were given sheep and tools and told never to make war. And so we've rebuilt our hogans and herded our sheep and lived the way the holy beings taught us to live in the beginning. We lived in the Rainbow Circle and followed the path of pollen. But the white man's government hadn't finished interfering with the Indians. They didn't know that we live within our sacred mountains—that we really shared the land with the Hopis. In 1882, President Chester Arthur signed an executive order that set aside two and one-half million acres for the use of the Hopis and any other Indians that the Secretary of Interior saw fit to settle there. That two and one-half million acres became known as the Joint Use Area. Many of our people had already lived there for generations. The Hopis and the Navajos were trying to live in peace as neighbors around the Female Mountain.

We're related also because we live upon the same Earth, our Mother, the Female Mountain, which starts from the tips of all the mesas, First, Second, Third and Howell Mesa, and it goes northward, and it forms Black Mesa. And then you get in toward Navajo Mountain, and all that area, including Navajo Mountain, is a woman's body, known as the Female Mountain. Navajo Mountain is the head. When the Hopis and Dineh people came to this world, they had their stories of where the Hopis come from, where the Dineh people come from, and how they come to meet at the foot of Female Mountain. And the *Yei* came and told both people, the Hopi and Dineh, to live there. The Hopis were guided to all their sacred springs and their sacred shrines. Many of them are where Dineh people live, in Black Mesa and Navajo Mountain and Big Mountain. And so that's how we're related. We're just one people, even though we have different languages.

After a while, the white man's government began to build schools on our land to teach us how to think like the white man.

Back in the late '60s, early '70s, when I was going to BIA school, things were pretty much like a prison. There were times when we couldn't speak our language, and if people would hear us speak Dineh in our school, we would be punished. We were taught in those schools how to disrespect one another. And as you began to get higher in the grades, you began to lose respect for home. Then when you get into high school, things are pretty different. By that time, you're just westernized; you're just already living the white man's ways and all. You learn the greed. They have a history. It's hard to point to where it all started. Where did all that greed and all that murderous thought come from? Just a loss of respect for the natural survival and the natural existence that they were supposed to live with. But that's the kind of thought there is. It doesn't have any meaning. It just brings contamination, corruption, sickness. A race of people with their minds gone.

In the 1930s the government drew its own line around the Hopi mesas and villages. Inside that line were 640,000 acres, and the white man called it the Hopi Reservation. Washington made the Navajos and Hopis form tribal councils to govern the Indian peoples. These councils had nothing to do with traditions of the Hopi or the Dineh. They were put there for the benefit of the government in Washington, to help the march of progress. Little signs began to appear in the BIA schools that said, "Tradition is the enemy of progress." Already the government was trying to relocate the minds of the Dineh into the ways of the white man.

Already, there's so much power of the white man that is on the reservation. And the power of the white man is being carried out by our own people, the Dineh people.

They always say, "I don't know. We have to call Washington."

In 1962 Washington said the Dineh couldn't build any more hogans in the Joint Use Area. Already the monster was getting hungry to eat the coal in the body of the Female Mountain. A few years later, Washington set up negotiations between the Hopi and Navajo Tribal Councils, and the Peabody Coal Company, who started to strip mine the coal on Black Mesa to make electricity to power the monster. The Navajo and Hopi traditional people strongly opposed the strip mining on Black Mesa. They came together to try to stop the monster from eating the heart of the Female Mountain. And it was in 1972 that a voice of the monster first spoke to the government in Washington, telling the government to divide the land in the JUA between the Hopis and the Navajos. The idea was to keep the Navajos and the Hopis from uniting against the government.

Back in 1974, I guess, in Washington, D.C., Congress voted on relocation of Navajo people in the Southwest of the United States. Our Tribal Councilmen never told us until 1977. We noticed that they were fencing, going around the areas that we live in. So finally it came into Big Mountain in late fall. And then people started wondering what was going on. And we found out that there was a land dispute between Hopis and Navajos—supposed to be, but there wasn't.

The land dispute is an invention of the white man's government. Public law 93.531, which would relocate 10,000 Navajos, is an invention of the white man's government. The land dispute is being negotiated by two Tribal Councils which are also inventions of the white man's government. The truth is this: The land dispute is just a trick the government is working on the Hopis and the Dineh to get the people to move off the land, so the monster can eat the minerals buried in the heart of the Female Black Mountain.

And a lot of things have been planned on this area; that's the mining of uranium or oil, whatever comes up. They're going to start destroying our medicines. This is the main point . . . we can't give up. As long as I'm here, I'm not going to give up. According to our old ancestors, they said, "Don't ever give up. There's something going to happen. It's going to be ruined some day. Either you're going to be shot, or whatever is going on. You're going to be destroyed first, and then they're going to destroy the land." We've been offering out here to the trees, to the hills, and to the spring and all that—we had our prayers set here, and we can't move and we can't break it. We'll just fight them if they try to force us.

In our religion, we have so many ways, and the prayers are in there, the laws are in there, the songs are all in there. We need to realize this thing and realize that the monster's intruding upon our land and that we need to be monster slayers. We need to be Dineh again. And then you have to live it; you have to live that way, how you pray; so if you say you're a monster slayer it has a lot of meaning. And it means that you're just a brother to the deer or a brother to the rabbit or the horny toads, or the eagle, or brother to the trees, and whatever grows on Mother Earth is our brother.

Why couldn't the white man just get away from it and have the Navajos and the Hopis just settle this whole thing?

The more you think about it, the American people, they're kind of brainwashed. I was married to a Hopi, and he and I used to really argue about this, because he wasn't really on his tribe's side. But in some ways, I probably made him angry by saying things, throwing this and that toward the Hopi. And he used to really get mad. And I used to get mad, because of what he was saying about the Navajos. They're using one tribe against the other; you read it in Indian history. It's been like that for centuries, and that's their favorite game.

My folks, the Dineh, have been in this area for generations upon generations. We have our own economics here; we have our own life-style here. And we have our own religion here. If we're told to move, we have our sacred mountain here. We can't move a sacred mountain. Anglos have a way of tearing down their temples and tearing down their churches and moving them elsewhere. But we cannot. That is not meant for us Native American Indians on this continent.

Since the government's always watching out for his own kind, why can't I look out for my own kind? I'm doing this for my children and their children's children. If I lose this, I have nothing to live for. What I'm thinking of it, is that big corporations are all behind it; and they know it too. Everybody knows that. They want to develop around here. They want to strip mine; because I've heard that there's oil and coal and uranium in this area. That's what they're really after. They're just using the Hopi people. I think the person that's really behind this is the Mormon people.

That's what relocation means to us—all those things—introduction of Christianity upon our land and forcing our young people to attend the BIA school and finally being educated to live the white man's life where they have to compete. People just have to resort to drinking or whatever—suicide. So that's—you know, relocation of the minds of the people, relocation of the spirit that once was the Dineh nation, that was once the pride of being a Dineh. That spirit is being relocated out of your physical being. The final step in relocation is physically removing people. They decided to just uproot the people, just take them out and just let them die like a tree without a root.

If your mother or grandparents were being moved out and being transplanted, do you think they will grow? No, I don't think so. I'm born just a little ways from here. My great-great-grandmother's buried on this site, just a little ways from where we've been herding sheep. And my great-grandmother is buried right across the canyon here. And my grandmother—I saw her when I was about six years old; she died and she's buried on the south side up here. And from her children are buried here. And us grandkids—my sister and brothers are buried around here, too. And my children, and also my grandchildren. So I just couldn't say I'm going to leave or I need to be relocated. I can't do it. My roots are just about that deep, maybe three or four down deep. So I can't be pulled out. This means you've got to move without your sheep, without your horses. I want to live here as long as I live. I still have sheep and horses, so I don't want to leave my sacred songs and prayers.

In 1981 the Navajo and Hopi Tribal Councils took jurisdiction of the former Joint Use Area. Relocation of the Dineh began when the monster started to give them money to move away from their sacred land. The old people, especially, didn't understand what it meant to be relocated. The monster said that maybe elders could remain on the land until they died, but that their kids would have to move on. They called this the "life estate."

It seems like they just wanted us to die real soon, or something like that.

But right now, there's no re-evaluation since the law was passed, and since the President of the United States had signed. There is no follow-up of what it is doing, how it is affecting the people. Probably somebody in the office just picks up a phone, says, "Everything is fine." But it's not fine. Right deep in the heart of whatever the law was made for is up in Big Mountain; and many people feel bad, and many people oppose, object to this law. Why do the Senators and Congressmen not have ears? Or are they too busy with something overseas that is on their conscience, that things like this are happening right in their backyards? And why can't these people have a little more thought to the people that were here when they first came?

Sometimes you think it's no use to be existing. It's no use. Everything you think about, it's just no use because something's there. You know, you're not supposed to improve yourself; you're not supposed to even keep yourself clean, your home clean, because somebody said no. How long are we Navajo going to take that? For me, I can not tolerate that. I'll have some way to strike back. You know, that's the only thing I'm thinking about. I'm starting to make plans how I'm going to strike back. I'm so mad, a lot of the time. And you know, I think my temperature is rising.

Well, you just get homesick, lonely and then worry too much and can't eat and you just get sick and die. That's all. That's the end of it. These old people had died just recently along the Dinebito trading post. And even across here, these neighbors, there's a lady that died of heart attack or something like that. Is this from that, too? And before she died her son shot himself. Because "I've got no land and I've got no place to go; I might as well do this." So he shot himself. See, this is what's happening. And some people hung themselves, around the neck, to a trading post. Three of them have done that.

If you're a believer of the tribal government, a government is supposed to take care of the people. And if you're a believer in that, then is that what the government is doing? Are they meeting the needs of the people? Why is there suicide? Why are the young people drinking and getting in wrecks along the highways? Is that a beautiful life? Is it a beautiful life if our young people are stuck in the agency towns, or border towns, being away from their parents while their parents are getting old and they can't get up fast enough to go turn the sheep back? We hardly think of those things, because the BIA has taken those kind of thoughts away from us. Today we're at a point where our own people are enemies. And our own people have gone through all these institutions.

This monster is the Federal Government of the United States again. I know a lot of American Indians. Their land has been stolen. This doesn't belong to the Federal Government. This doesn't belong to the Navajo Tribal Council. This belongs to us. This land is ours. It doesn't belong to Federal Government; it doesn't belong to the Navajo Tribal Council.

It seems like there's a turning point, for people to return to the Dineh way or just go the ways of the White man, where we live in a materialistic world, and there's no connection to the Earth or the universe. It's a long ways to educate ourselves again. We need to consult with our elders and say, "What should be the goal?"

And I would say to the youth people, or younger generation on the Navajo Reservation, to get their heads together and start thinking, start making sense.

Our responsibility as young Dineh people is to secure the future for our elders and for ourselves and the future generation. The only hope is the new generation, the young people. As far as the elders, there's unity. We've lived with the Hopis for many centuries; and they come up on our land to gather wood and to trade with our people and to socialize with our people. And that's how we've always lived. We still live that way. And we want to continue to live that way. And the Dineh from the beginning were given a prayer, a song, and many different songs for different ways. And in those prayers, we identify ourselves to the natural surroundings, the natural forces—the wind, the rain and the sun, the universe and the earth. And so we're right there, the human beings, the five-fingered beings. So our people constantly keep the same mind, because they know every day they greet the sun. They greet the twilight and the morning. They greet the Big Dipper; the universe; the Little Dipper. And they identify themselves who they are, the Dineh people, the Hopi people. Because it's all said in the prayers, as the Twin Warriors, when they went to kill the monsters that were an enemy to the people, that were destroying all the people. My people in Big Mountain have finally made a stand to resist. We want to continue that way and resist as much as we can, as peacefully as we can against the BIA, the Tribal Government, the Tribal Police, and the Federal Government. It's all the same thing, the same monster. It just has all the tentacles, this monster. We are the Twin Warriors, we are the Monster Slayers. Being a warrior doesn't just mean a man. It means a woman, too.

Well, I'll just load up my gun and then walk out toward them if they start coming to me. I had my heart beating kind of strong all the time, so I know I don't have any fear; so I think that we're going to win to have our land back.

Kill the monster!

This monster is a state of mind, which is attacking us, the Dineh. To resist this monster, we must remember who we are. We must listen to our elders, to learn from them again and again the truth of what it means to be a Dineh. We must grow strong in our spirits. We must think clearly with our minds. We must have perfect health in our bodies. We must always carry the truth of the Navajo tradition in our hearts. In this way, we will be able to recognize the monster when it tries to sneak into and amongst ourselves. If we are strong, we will refuse to be relocated from our tradition into the ways of the monster. We will refuse to be relocated from our homeland around the Female Mountain. We will not take money from the monster for our land. Because money is a weapon of the monster that disappears fast from our hands. We will defend ourselves by refusing to participate in the ways of the monster. We will obey the laws of our tradition. We are a nation of Dineh. Our greatest weapon is the spirit of our people. And our spirit will destroy the monster that has invaded Dinetah. Our war is not with the Hopi people. Our war is with the monster that has crept into the hearts of some of the Hopi and some of the Navajos and made them blind to who they really are. With our tradition we will stop the progress of this monster in Dinetah.

STEWART UDALL

*STEWART UDALL AND HIS FAMILY have been friends of mine
for many years. One time as we were driving through
northern New Mexico, Stewart told me that he had started
out as a conservationist of the Teddy Roosevelt school
and that through the course of his lifetime his
environmental awareness had gone through many
permutations. In 1963 Stewart's book,* The Quiet Crisis, *was
published and introduced many Americans to the fact that
we were facing a form of jeopardy that had been perceived by
very few.*

*Stewart Udall was appointed Secretary of the Interior by
President John F. Kennedy, an office he held for eight years,
through the end of the Johnson administration. Prior to his
tenure in the Cabinet, he was a U.S. Congressman from
Arizona, where he was born. Through the 1970s and '80s
Stewart has practiced environmental law, often on behalf of
Navajo uranium miners and their widows, and he has written
more books and articles, including* To the Inland Empire. *He
is currently preparing a history of the nuclear age.*

*Stewart Udall, along with historians Alvin Josephy and Bill
Brown, taught me the importance of perceiving past events
within their historic contexts, that one cannot clearly isolate*

an event from its continuum. Hence the old adage,
"Hindsight is greater than foresight."
  Stewart is in a unique position to discuss the history of
what has happened at Black Mesa and Big Mountain.

———

JACK LOEFFLER   I wonder if you could give a sense of the nature
of the 1960s and the whole system of coordinates that prevailed
with regard to energy production at that time and the need for
energy in the future?

STEWART UDALL   Well, to be very honest with you, I think that
we made a series of spectacular miscalculations back in the 1950s
and 1960s. I suppose it is a confessional, in a sense, to say that. I
think that we felt there was no energy problem. The energy problem had been solved by science and technology. Optimism about
atomic power was really at the center of things in that period.
We also had made some very bad misjudgments about how much
oil and gas we had in this country. We almost treated them as
though they weren't finite, nonrenewable sources, but that we
would go on and find more and more, and that we had another
hundred years, two hundred years of oil. The whole atmosphere
of the 1950s, 1960s was not to worry, there were no problems,
we were so clever, and we were such masters of science and technology that shortages had been eliminated for all time.

JL   Could you give some background to this history of what led
up to coal extraction in the area around Black Mesa, Arizona?

SU   I often wondered, when I look back at the 1960s, to what
extent the Hopis themselves really ever sat down and decided
what they wanted to do with their resources. I know what
the attitude of the traditional Hopis was, and that was anti-
development. Leave it alone.

  You know, there's only one part of Arizona where oil has been
found, and that's in the Four Corners area. The Black Mesa basin,
which drains to the Colorado to the south, at one point was

thought to be highly promising as an oil province, and the question was, would the tribes approve oil leasing? The Navajos, of course, had already set a precedent. They had struck oil, and that oil supposedly made them wealthy Indians in the 1950s. That was one of the myths of the Navajos—that they were wealthy Indians. The Hopis, however, had no experience with oil. And my recollection is that oil leases were approved, and that there was some drilling done in the Black Mesa basin. They didn't find any oil and gas, but that represented a kind of threshhold decision in the Hopi country.

JL   Can you describe how the Hopi Tribal Council, as we currently know it, came to exist?

SU   I've never studied the subject of Hopi politics in the last forty years in an intense way. Some of the studying I did do, though, led me to the fascinating conclusion which, to me at least, demonstrates the extent to which some of us non-Indians, who thought of ourselves as being pro-Indian and wanted to be helpful and so on, participated in things we wondered about or questioned later. You know, there never was a Hopi tribe. As I understand their history, they're a group of clans, and to superimpose a tribal government on them was, in effect, using our way of thinking in a rigid approach. But the person who went to the Hopi, and who persuaded them to vote to establish a tribal government, was Oliver LaFarge. I don't think anyone would say that Oliver LaFarge, in terms of his own intentions, didn't have the best thoughts in mind as far as the Indians were concerned. But he participated in that. It was set up.

That was, of course, where the split between the traditionals and progressives came out into the open, way back in the 1930s. But once they set up a government, and then the traditionals said, "This does not represent our culture, and we won't participate in it," you had a schism there, and of course the progressives then had to have lawyers, like John Boyden, who had their own attitude toward development. The extent to which they were

pushed by the Bureau of Indian Affairs, the extent to which someone like John Boyden pushed them, because his attitudes were
pro-development, as I'm sure they were, I don't know. I suspect
that yes, they were pushed.

JL   One of the questions that has come up in a lot of people's
minds centered around Norman Littel. Could you give some sense
of how that whole situation came to be, why he had to be fired?

SU   Well, Littel was like John Boyden, a very strong-minded individual, in fact more so. He had been an assistant attorney general under Franklin D. Roosevelt and was a very arrogant man.
In fact Roosevelt had to fire him personally, call him on the phone
and say, "You're fired!" It's a famous story.

When he became the attorney for the Navajos right after World
War II, as I recall, he became a very dominating, domineering
influence. Then, as now, the Tribal Chairman and the little group
around him had great power. But the Tribal Chairmen at that
time were not educated men in terms of our world, and so Littel
was very manipulative. He and I parted company and had a rather
bitter ending to what had been a working relationship after I
became Secretary of the Interior. Littel made the decisions himself, and then he would gather the Chairmen around and give
them the impression that they were making the decision. In the
election in the early 1960s, when Raymond Nakai was elected,
he sensed that Littel was bad news for the tribe, and he said, "If
you elect me, I'll get rid of him." He won the election against
Paul Jones. But Littel wouldn't go. In fact he had secretly written long-term contracts. I told him he had to go, that he had got
involved in their politics, and that the new Chairman ought to
be able to select his own man. That ended in a bitter fight that
went all the way through the courts for five or six years. They
finally ruled in my favor, as Secretary of Interior.

JL   To what extent would you hazard that both the Navajo
and Hopi Tribal Councils were constructed to function as

organizations to deal with the United States Government on behalf of their respective tribes?

SU Do you mean deal with their resources, or deal as a government?

JL Deal as a government. Here the emphasis is to try to determine to what extent the government ultimately is responsible for some of the situations which are still being felt today, like relocation, for example. To what extent were the Tribal Councils established because the government needed somebody to talk to in order to legalize their own relationship to the tribes?

SU Well, one has to go back and study the evolution of the political and governmental institutions that we imposed on them. Because in the beginning, when we recognized in at least the Southwest that they would be allowed to keep land and have reservations where they supposedly were in command of things, the idea was, "We'll leave you alone, and you go ahead and govern yourselves." One of the most fascinating documents was the treaty with the Navajo Indians. They stopped making treaties with Indians soon after that. The essential philosophy of that treaty, when you read it, was: "Well, you're back from the Long Walk now, and if you will be peaceful and you will not create problems, we will respect your right to make decisions." At that time, of course, the Navajo Indian culture itself had its own way of identifying leadership. Our idea was a tribal council and elections. Theirs, as I understand their history, was based on their own culture and their own tradition, and usually this included elders and head men and concepts of that kind. And so for a long time, to the extent that decisions had to be made—for example, a railroad being built through northern Arizona, water rights and other things of that kind—the Indians lacked the capacity to understand what the white man was doing, and the extent that it impinged on his resources, and his future. In that beginning period, up until the time that tribal governments were started under Franklin D. Roosevelt, Indian agents, as they were called, were very powerful men. They had more power, really, than the elders and leaders of Indian groups. That was a long phase, perhaps in some instances five or six decades. I can remember, even in my own lifetime, when the superintendent at Navajo was really the person that made these big decisions where the United States Government and our development industries had an interest in the resources of an Indian reservation.

JL   The *Healing vs. Jones* decision was made . . .

SU   About that time, the time I became Secretary . . . in fact that was the decision on the partition, the boundary decision, wasn't it?

JL   Yes it was. It has been said that that decision was basically a manipulation by outside interests to determine who owned the land so that contracts regarding energy could be signed with the Indians, or with whoever owned the land. Would you regard that as a true statement?

SU   Well, that probably was lurking in the background. When I was a Congressman in the 1950s, there wasn't the pressure between the two tribes that existed twenty years later, with the enormous population growth of the Navajo Tribe. Whereas the Hopis, with a slower population growth rate, were able to accommodate themselves. It was really the population pressure of the Navajos, and their "expansionism," you might say, that forced some of the issues to the forefront out there. I may have been wrong, but I always thought, as a Congressman, that the Federal Government had fouled up in the beginning when the two reservations were set up. As far as the Indian Bureau and the United States Government were concerned, everybody sort of looked the other way, hoping the problem would go away. And it wasn't until the late 1950s and 1960s that pressures began to build up for a settlement, for a definition of where the boundaries were. That later led to the present controversy over land rights and who should be where, and so on.

JL   Do you recall the names of the participants, or the members of the consortium known as West and Associates?

SU   West, the energy group? This was something that developed before I became Secretary of Interior, in the late 1950s. As I became acquainted with it later, it developed out of a desire by the big power companies in Albuquerque, Phoenix, Los Angeles, who were all working together on this, to develop additional energy resources in the Southwest region. It was interesting that they began to look at coal. Coal use was declining in the eastern part of the United States after World War II. Coal, for a while, was a dying industry. It was being replaced by cheap oil as fuel for electric power generation plants.

Suddenly in the West, because of peculiar conditions that existed here, because the air pollution was as it was in Southern California, the power companies were under pressure not to burn oil or anything that polluted. So they began looking at nuclear power. They began looking at reaching outside their own region, into the Southwest, and using coal. And suddenly coal, for that reason, became a resource that the power companies wanted to develop. So they teamed up. West was a planning group, and essentially one organization. Arizona Public Service, or whoever it might be, would build the plant. Others would own parts of the plant and put up the capital to build it. That's where the original coal development, the Four Corners power plant came from, which was probably the most horrible polluter in the United States. It's the one that the astronauts saw and photographed from outer space. That was well underway when I became Secretary of the Interior in 1961. Of course, the attitude by pro-development people was, "This is a good thing, because we are developing the Indians' resources and this will help them."

JL   Do you think that the pro-development people might have been lobbying to influence the *Healing vs. Jones* decision? Or had they been lobbying one tribe or the other in those days?

SU   I'm not all that familiar with the relations these companies had with Norman Littel, the lawyer for the Navajos, for example. I'm sure they dealt with him. And he had, of course, his own ideas. As I recall, he was pro-development regarding Indian resources. They must have been lobbying because of the success that they had in putting these various projects through, and because you had to get some kind of rubber-stamp approval from a tribal council. This could be done by the Bureau of Indian Affairs, by an attorney like Littel or Boyden, and by some persuasion or arm-twisting with the little groups that were the elected leaders of Indian tribes at that time.

JL   It's been said that John Boyden was affiliated with a public relations firm in Salt Lake City known as Evans and Associates, who also represented other interests—namely, the Peabody Coal Company—and that Boyden, himself, might actually have been serving two interests at the same time—namely the Hopi tribe and the Peabody Coal Company. Does that sound at all correct to you?

SU   Well, I learned this long afterwards. In fact, I learned it for the first time just a few years ago, and I was rather taken aback. I always thought Boyden, because he was the Mormon elder kind of person, was, within his own lights, an honest man. And this would have said that he was engaged in some questionable and devious activities, and that maybe his main interest was representing other clients—that he had a conflict of interest. Because he had to run the approval that was obtained for the Black Mesa coal development through the tribal government that existed at that time. But if he was simultaneously being paid by the Peabody Coal Company, this is what we would call a very blatant conflict of interest in white man's society, by any standard.

JL   Wasn't he paid a million dollars by the Hopi tribe, finally, for having represented them through all of that?

SU   I never did get into those details. All that came out in the 1970s, after I was there, but I'm sure he was well paid. In fact, Littel was well paid. There were decisions made that involved tens and hundreds of millions of dollars, and in some instances they wrote contracts with the Indians that were favorable to themselves. This is one of the big arguments that Littel and I had. He had an outrageous contract with them that he was going to get a percentage, in *Healing vs. Jones,* of the minerals from the land that the Navajos ended up with as a result of the litigation, or the action by Congress, to resolve this. And he would have had that. This was unconscionable. The Indian lawyers didn't have contracts like that, and he knew it and I knew it. That was one of the things that he did that made me angry. I went to court as a witness only one time in my eight years as Secretary of the Interior. You don't have to, usually; you can send a deputy or someone. But I went to court on the Littel case. The judge was John Sirica. I didn't know him then, he wasn't famous then—Watergate fame. He apparently was a friend of Littel, and he chose to believe Littel and to disbelieve me. We had to appeal his verdict and get it reversed.

JL   I wonder if you could describe what the Central Arizona Project really means, and how that might be related to mineral extraction on the reservation?

SU   Well, the states of the Colorado River Basin got together with Herbert Hoover as the arbiter and divided up the waters of the river and then drew up plans for development. Arizona was to get a substantial share of the water of the Colorado as a lower basin state through which the river drained. That became a fifty-year fight—for Arizona to get its share—for all of us that were involved in Arizona politics. Almost in a knee-jerk way, we were anti-California, we were pro-Arizona water development, and I worked on that as a Congressman. I worked on it as Secretary of Interior. I guess the main thing that motivated us was a matter of fairness—because Los Angeles had been using Arizona's water for forty years, yet there was a compact between the states, ratified by Congress, saying that this was Arizona's water. Now the only direct way that this had an impact on Indian resources—I guess you could talk about two things. One was Glen Canyon Dam, which flooded a lot of Indian land. There's no question about that. The other was the Page power plant which was built to use Black Mesa coal. There's a train that takes the coal over there. They drew an arbitrary line at Glen Canyon, which separated the upper basin and the lower basin, and they assigned to the State of Arizona, in that agreement, fifty or sixty thousand acre-feet of water, as an upper basin state. That was just a contract, it was just a piece of paper. That water had never been put to use, and there were no plans to put it to use. Somebody came up with the smart idea that the water should be used for the coal-fired power plant at Page, Arizona.

There's a fascinating history that I'll deal with briefly in that connection. In Bureau of Reclamation projects you always had to build a hydroelectric dam. The hydroelectric dams which were originally planned as part of Arizona's water project were two dams in what is now the Grand Canyon—Marble Canyon and Bridge Canyon. The Sierra Club and others, for very good conservation reasons, opposed those dams. And my friend Dave Brower (he doesn't like to talk about it much now) in the middle 1960s was saying, "Don't build these dams. Build a nuclear power plant." Nuclear power at that time was marching under the banner of clean energy, cheap energy, and conservationists like myself and Brower were not opposed to it. So in effect, when I decided that the dams should not be built, we had to have another power source. It either had to be a nuclear power plant or it had to be a coal plant. Nuclear power was not sufficiently advanced at that time. So that idea was passed over.

Some of the Arizona people and some of the power companies got busy and put together this Page Power Plant. The Federal Government owns part of it—we broke the mold with that plant. It will supply the energy to pump the water out of the Colorado River and into Phoenix and Tucson. So there's a very direct connection there, as you can see. It'll be Indian coal providing the energy to pump the water into the central valleys of Arizona.

JL   Who negotiated for the 34,000 acre-feet of water to cool that plant?

SU   This was the subject that I mentioned earlier—this was the supposedly "unused" Arizona allocation of the mainstream flow of the river. We're not talking about groundwater. This is the mainstream flow of the river. That water was allocated for that purpose. And I had to approve that. I have to take some responsibility for it, because I had my own dilemmas. Once I was convinced that it was a bad policy to put dams in the Grand Canyon, and that you could never get Congress to approve it, the whole Central Arizona Project would have failed if you didn't have an energy source. The idea that some of the people came up with was the coal-fired power plant that was ultimately built.

JL   I'm now thinking in terms of the result of the *Healing vs. Jones* decision regarding the dividing line between Hopi and Navajo. Do you have any recollection as to which side of that line possesses more extractable resources?

SU   I've never studied it in that light. Congress really concentrated on this in 1974. I was long gone by then. But Black Mesa is one of the main geographic features of that region, and of course it drains as a basin into the Little Colorado River. It was known all along that there was high quality coal there. As I said earlier, there was also some feeling at one time that there might be a big oil field in the Black Mesa Basin. And the area where the coal is, is also in the disputed area.

JL   As a result of an act of Congress, a large number of Navajos who are now living in what has been determined to be Hopi-owned land in the former Joint Use Area are to be relocated. What are your feelings about that?

SU   I have very mixed feelings. Any time people have deep roots in a part of the land, as those Indians do, and you force them to relocate, it's a very tragic, painful thing. So you have to regret that. On the other hand, confronted with a very large and vigorous tribe like the Navajos and a small and rather peaceful tribe like the Hopis, I don't know if we had left them to their own devices, if we hadn't come into the region, whether the problem would ever have existed. They might have simply resolved it in their own way. But once we got this into a legal framework, and we began having courts look at it, and we began having Congress look at it—where was the boundary? Where was it intended to be?—it then became a legalistic proposition. And, because it involves these King Solomon decisions, I'm rather glad that it didn't come up while I was Secretary of the Interior. I'm not sure that any decision isn't in some respect wrong, in terms of the people themselves. I can see both sides of it. I could see both sides of it when I was a Congressman. I think that it might have been resolved much more easily if it had been tackled back in the 1950s or early 1960s by just leaving people where they were and figuring out some way to paper it over. But now we have given the Indians, through laws and so on, our own legalistic framework of land ownership, of boundaries, things of that kind. And then we pitch them right into our kind of disputes.

JL   In retrospect, would you have approached anything differently regarding the Southwest and the whole business of energy extraction?

SU   Well, I don't have any great feelings of guilt or of having made wrong decisions or anything with regard to the period in the 1960s, although my attitude has changed. You know, our attitudes then were, "Gee whiz, coal is a resource that doesn't appear to have a future in this country. Indians have coal, so if you can develop your resources, they get some benefits out of it." This was the white man's attitude. You were doing a good thing for them to help develop their resources. I knew quite a bit, but not nearly as much as I do now, about Indian attitudes toward land and resources. I do have some feelings that we made some mistakes, that we pushed too hard and that decisions were made by whites, and then given the appearance of Indian decisions when actually there was a lot of pressure and manipulation and maneuvering.

I now have even stronger feelings than I had then about this whole business of the long view with regard to resources. I'm appalled at Watt,[1] for example, who seems to be bent on inviting other countries from abroad into the U.S. You know, the United States has turned its back on nuclear power, yet there are German and French companies moving into the Arizona strip to mine uranium. They don't have uranium in their countries. He's now talking about letting Kuwait and other Arab countries come in and develop our resources for extraction. I'm kind of reactionary, I guess, in that respect. I think that any country ought to be essentially self-sufficient in terms of food production. I think as far as energy is concerned that countries ought to be—for the long haul—substantially self-sufficient and try to conduct a society and a relationship with resources that have a long-term future. But these attitudes have formed in my mind, I'd say, in the last ten years, particularly since OPEC. In that sense, one of the things I admire about the current group of Indian leaders is the go-slow approach toward the development of their own resources. A lot of people are saying now, "They have uranium, they have coal and so on, but they're not helping the country by developing their resources." Well, if they want to go slow, particularly now that they have a lot more say than they had in the 1960s, I think that's their business, and that maybe going slow is a good thing for them and for the country as a whole, when you look at the long-term future.

JL   What is your philosophy with regard to nuclear energy at this point?

---

1. At the time of this interview Watt was still Secretary of the Interior under President Reagan.

SU   Well, since I left the President's Cabinet in 1969 I've essentially turned 180 degrees. I was one of those who sort of marched along meekly to the beat of the nuclear drummers, thought that this was a great thing. We could do it and there were no problems. It was the wave of the future. Now I see the negative side of nuclear energy and I am working on lawsuits that involve the horrible mistakes and the human debris that were left out of the 1950s—the Navajo uranium miners I represent, the people that were harmed by the fallout from the Nevada bombs, and things of that kind. I see very clearly how adroitly they brushed the problems under the rug, and when they were saying "safe, clean," we accepted it in the 50s and 60s because we didn't understand. We didn't think we could understand. They were an elite, and these were the great men. They were constructing this brave new world of the future, and we just had to go along with it. I see this all now as a mistake, and I'm going to write a book on this history of it, at least as I recall it and as I see it now.

JOHN FIFE

FOR THREE MILLENIA the act of providing asylum for those who are persecuted has been practiced by religious organizations. The concept of sanctuary may have had its genesis in ancient Egypt. It is known to have been practiced throughout European history, with one infamous exception, in the first half of the 20th century.

Since the early 1980s, the Sanctuary movement has gained fair momentum in the United States. Members of Sanctuary provide asylum for political refugees from El Salvador and Guatemala, where the U.S. Government, under the Reagan Administration, greatly escalated military aid to members of the ruling oligarchies.

In 1981 the Reverend John Fife of the United Presbyterian Church of South Tucson, Arizona, opened the doors of his church to political refugees from El Salvador and Guatemala, challenging all Americans to carefully examine the motives of our government and ourselves.

In 1985, John Fife and ten other people were indicted for providing sanctuary to political refugees. In October of 1985, these eleven people were brought to trial before Judge Earl Carroll. John Fife was ultimately sentenced to five years probation, which means that he can't have a gun, can't vote, *can't go south of the border to Mexico or Central America. To date, the Reverend Fife still provides sanctuary to political refugees, people who are forced to flee their homes because of grim political conditions that exist in their homelands, conditions imposed largely by the presence of representatives of the United States Government who are more concerned with protecting vested interests than with allowing Third World cultures to evolve unhampered.*

JACK LOEFFLER   What do you know of U.S. involvement in Central America that has contributed to these refugees seeking Sanctuary here?

JOHN FIFE   Well, that's a very complex question, and we won't know the complete picture for ten or fifteen years. But we know enough to know that the United States Government is involved in a deliberate military policy resulting in the creation of millions of refugees in El Salvador and Guatemala in order to maintain the oligarchy and the military that has ruled those unfortunate nations for fifty years now. That policy is designed to dislocate people from their homes, their family, the land, the community—to drive them into refugee camps. The United States Government calls them "model villages" now in El Salvador. We called them "strategic hamlets" in Vietnam when we were pursuing the same military policy there. These places are controlled by the government and the army, where the people are dependent for their food every day upon the army of El Salvador or Guatemala, where people can be removed at will and interrogated. It's a means of controlling the population through terror and even torture and death. That is a deliberate policy of the United States Government, imposed on the militaries of El Salvador and Guatemala. When the United States needed to design a military policy for El Salvador and Guatemala, they asked the Argentinian generals to come and show the Salvadorans how they did it in

Argentina, where they had tortured and murdered 30,000 during the most tragic period of Argentine history, with the full knowledge of the United States Government. We know that for certain. That was in massive violation of human rights.

We know now that the head of the death squads, Colonel Nicholas Carranza, was a CIA agent for five years before the death squads started, and was paid by the CIA as an agent during the entire time the death squads were operating in El Salvador. We know that Roberto D'Aubisson, the number two man in the death squad structure in El Salvador, responsible for the murder of at least 45,000 civilians now, was advised directly by even such institutions as the Republican National Committee on how to form a political wing for the death squad members, and to participate in elections which were going to be held. All of that we know.

Beyond that, we know that the U.S. Government has pumped $1.4 billion in aid to the military of El Salvador during that same period of time. We know that the military strategy is being directed by U.S. advisors, and that it is, literally, our war against the people of El Salvador and against the people of Guatemala, in order to maintain a system of rule by a tiny minority made up of military and oligarchy. The final part of that strategy is to "hold elections" for candidates who are acceptable to the United States and who will maintain that status quo as a kind of facade for justifying the massive murder, the massive dislocation of entire populations of people in both El Salvador and Guatemala—a clear genocidal campaign against the Indian population, the indigenous population of Guatemala, and to do all of this in the name of defending democracy and freedom.

JL   Has the counter-Sanctuary movement gained momentum since the 1984 presidential elections?

JF   Well, the counter-Sanctuary movement is not a movement at all. It's a deliberate attempt by the Immigration and Naturalization Service and the State Department to try to discredit the

Sanctuary movement and the churches and the people who are involved in this whole effort. It's being orchestrated out of Washington, D.C. It's very carefully planned, the information flow is very deliberate.

Here in Tucson there have been two parts to that. One is the indictments of priests, nuns, pastors, lay workers in the church, in an attempt to brand us as criminals, when the clear disobedience of law is on the part of this government every time it has arrested, detained, and deported a Salvadoran or a Guatemalan. It's in violation of international law, it's in violation of United States law, and they're simply trying through the indictments to give people the impression that it is pastors, priests and nuns who are criminals, and not the bureaucrats in Washington who send people back to their deaths. The response that they've got from the church community and the religious leadership in the United States, bishops and archbishops, from congregations across the United States, who are now declaring Sanctuary in record numbers in response to the indictments, all mean that it's a failure.

The second thing that they tried was to organize groups of people to be opposed to Sanctuary in their communities, and to give them information that would damage the Sanctuary movement. Here in Tucson they tried it, and they came up with five retired army colonels, one pastor of an independent church here, who acknowledged he had not asked his congregation whether he ought to be opposed to Sanctuary or not, and one American Legion Post, who gave them a letter saying that of course they were in favor of obedience to the law. That was it. When they met with the press to announce that they'd formed this organization against Sanctuary, they acknowledged that none of them had ever talked to a Central American refugee, that they didn't know the international law with regard to refugees, but, by golly, they were in favor of obedience to the law. We have no quarrel with that. We just wish the United States Government would start obeying the law, and there wouldn't be any life or death problem for Central American refugees at this point. I think that campaign is going to continue. I think it's going to be further heightened and become more frantic as the State Department and the Immigration and Naturalization Service find themselves more and more and more on the defensive, and that the kind of myths that they've created become more and more discredited. And I think that the public relations effort on the part of this administration, who use public relations efforts to bolster their own policies and discredit anybody who disagrees with them, will be an increasingly frantic kind of effort in the months to come.

JL What's the history of indictments with regard to the Sanctuary leaders?

JF The first indictments came in South Texas against Stacey Merkt and Jack Elder in February and March of 1984. Phil Conger, a church worker here in Tucson was indicted at the same time. That's been a part of a continuing strategy on the part of the Immigration and Naturalization Service and it might be helpful to review that strategy.

When we first declared Sanctuary, they developed a policy that would probably be described as benign neglect. "If we ignore them they'll go away; what's one dinky little Presbyterian Church down in South Tucson in Arizona gonna do to affect immigration and foreign policy in Central America?" That didn't work. The idea of Sanctuary caught on and churches began to declare Sanctuary in communities across the United States. They couldn't maintain that benign neglect policy anymore, so they tried to discredit us publicly. Spokesmen for INS have said, "Well, we have evidence that they're not really helping Salvadorans or Guatemalans at all. They're doing this media hype thing, and we're not sure who those people are, but we don't even think that they're undocumented Salvadorans or Guatemalans that are doing Sanctuary. It's just a public relations effort on the part of the churches." That's a strange thing to be coming from an administration who lives and dies on public relations, but, nevertheless, that's what they accused us of. That didn't work because we literally took scores of journalists along with us to the border, to Mexico, and said, "You just report on what you see and what you hear," and even took television cameras with us in some instances, so that our activity was well documented by journalists who certainly would have exposed us if we'd been doing anything other than what we said we were doing. The policy to discredit us failed.

Then they began to threaten prosecution of anybody in any of the churches found in violation of the law. And a year went by. Finally came the first indictments of Stacy and Jack in South Texas and of Phil here in Tucson. That was obviously an attempt to say, "Well, we'll take two or three of them to court, we'll get a conviction against them, and that'll put a stop to those church people who are doing Sanctuary." The response was overwhelming on the part of the churches in terms of support for Jack, Stacy and Phil, as well as a dramatic increase in the number of churches declaring Sanctuary. So that one failed. Now what you see is an attempt to indict sixteen people in Arizona, to take to court what government perceives to be the leaders of the Sanctuary movement, and see if that won't work. Their strategy obviously has been to increase the level of repression against the churches and church workers involved in the Sanctuary movement. In a way it's a kind of compliment by the government to our efforts. They couldn't afford to ignore us, because we were becoming more and more and more effective. Unfortunately, rather than choosing to change the policy in response to the will of the American people, they chose to hammer back and react in authoritarian and repressive ways. But that should not surprise us, either. That's been their response in Central America to what is clearly a movement by their people for liberation.

JL   I know that you have legal precedents in your favor. How does the Sanctuary movement fit within the context of the Geneva Convention and the U.S. Refugee Act of 1980?

JF   Well, we not only recognize those legal precedents, but so does the government. When they indicted us, the government filed a motion asking the judge to rule that we could not, in our defense, mention anything about international law, about United States refugee law, about conditions in El Salvador, about conditions in Guatemala, about our religious faith, or about the possible refugee status of the people we've been assisting. Now that's the only chance the government has. If they can keep us from talking about the law, United States law and international refugee law, then they may be able to convict us in a court—if a jury can't hear about the massive violations of the law by the United States Government. But the 1949 Geneva Accord on the treatment of refugees states that civilians have not only the right but the duty, and it uses the word "duty," to protect refugee populations when governments fail to do so for political reasons. That's the provision of international law we believe we've been operating under since 1981. We believe the government understands that as well. In addition to that, United States refugee law says, right at the heart of it, that under no circumstances does the United States have the right to deport a refugee back to a place where his life might be threatened or he might be under fear of prosecution upon his return. That's illegal, and the United States has been doing that—deporting people recognized as refugees by the United Nations, by Amnesty International, by America's Watch, by the OAS Human Rights Commission, for five years now. They have been violating the law and violating the common humanity of the people of Central American by deporting people back to a place where their lives are indeed threatened and to a place where many of them have lost their lives because of that deportation process.

JL Has Sanctuary been infiltrated by government informants?

JF Yes. When they began the indictments against Jack and Stacy and Phil in South Texas and Arizona, we kept saying, "This is just preparation for a crackdown against the Sanctuary movement. You all need to understand that." The government in all its public statements said, "Aw, that's silly. We're not planning a crackdown against the Sanctuary movement. We're not anticipating anything like that. It's simply not one of our priorities." At the same time, for the ten months they were making those statements, they knew that they had paid INS agents and two paid informers inside the church, inside Bible study groups, inside church meetings, inside worship services of the church, with wireless transmitters on, transmitting what was being said and what was going on in those Bible study groups and church meetings, to vans parked outside the church where all that was being recorded. They also volunteered to transport refugees in the Phoenix community to Bible study groups in a Lutheran church held every Sunday night for refugees and North Americans who wanted to study together. That way they obtained the addresses of refugees living in the Phoenix area and used that to pick up forty-seven of them when we were indicted on January 15th.

The fundamental question that underlies all of this, of course, is what kind of people are we, and what kind of values and traditions characterize us as Americans generally, and as Christian Americans, or as Jewish Americans or as Unitarian Americans, or as humanitarian Americans here in this country? Those questions underlie this whole subject—what in the world is our government doing in Central America? What in the world are we doing with regard to refugees from that terror-stricken land? That fundamental question is going to be answered over the next year or two by the people. What we're trying to do is keep that question before them with as much integrity as we can muster on our own, as congregations and as individuals in our ministry, and to say we're willing to run risks in order to maintain what we had assumed all along were clearly understood and deeply held values and traditions. If we fail to answer that with our traditional values, then I think we have not only lost our identity as Americans, as Christians, as Jews, as Unitarians, as humanitarians, but we've probably given up our souls as well.

It's just that critical. It's one of those times in history when you've either got to give up everything that you've always believed and sell your soul, or stand firm and reaffirm those ethical and moral values that we hold to be sacred. I think that's the question. All the rest of it is detail, but it drives you inevitably to that fundamental question. The answer, the outcome, is going to be a very interesting time for us all.

DOUGLAS PEACOCK

THE DAY AFTER THANKSGIVING in 1975, Douglas Peacock and I were sitting in my living room in northern New Mexico. I had just spotted a black bear climbing the hill on the opposite side of the canyon. Peacock had been telling me about his forays into grizzly bear country armed with a 16-mm movie camera. I had seen some of his footage; I recalled one shot in particular—a great, browsing grizzly bear Peacock had filmed from thirty to forty feet away.

"Peacock," says I, "that looks like a good way to get mauled."

"You gotta be careful," says Peacock.

"How careful can you be when you're thirty feet from a grizzly bear and half a mile from the nearest tree?" says I.

"You gotta be real careful," says Peacock.

Since that day, Douglas has written a book entitled The Grizzly Years, *which melds his experience as a Vietnam vet with his tireless attempt to defend the rights of grizzly bears in the contiguous forty-eight states. He was the subject of a documentary film entitled* Peacock's War, *which was shown on PBS. Peacock has lectured throughout the United States on the plight of the grizzly, which, curiously enough, is the plight of all living creatures who participate in the flow of Nature.*

JACK LOEFFLER   Doug, can you describe when you started becoming aware of your affinity with grizzly bears?

DOUGLAS PEACOCK   Well, I'd seen a grizzly twenty-five years ago in Alaska. I was up on a tundra on some kind of paleontological grant from the National Science Foundation. I was twenty years old and a big punk kid, and I carried a .44 magnum. I actually saw a grizzly and had one charge across the tundra toward me. I got my old piece out there and the bear ambled up within about fifteen yards and just took off again. I knew after a couple of seconds I wasn't going to blow the bear away anyway.

That was the first time I ever saw a grizzly, but, you know, it didn't take that first time. I didn't realize what I was dealing with. It probably wasn't until seven or eight years later when I came back from Vietnam that griz really took with me. I camped out for a couple of years when I came back in the late '60s. Like a lot of other vets I was out of sorts. I wasn't much good with people and essentially didn't have a serious conversation for two years. I camped out. In the winter time I camped out here in the desert or went down to Baja or Sonora, and when the snows melted I'd go up to the Wind River and up to the Yellowstone country.

And the Yellowstone country is where I first ran into grizzly. One of the places where I camped a lot happened to be a place where grizzlies congregated in those days. I'd see fifteen or twenty grizzlies every day. I recall one of the first grizzlies I saw. I happened to be camped beside a little hot creek that starts out boiling and dumps into a river a couple of miles away, where it's tepid. In between you've got every temperature of water you want. I'd just got over a malaria attack and was feeling weak, so I was going to go bask and soak in the hot waters for a while to regain my health, get my strength back.

I was sitting in one of these really hot pools in this little creek one day, and across the meadow came a sow grizzly with a couple of cubs. She was only about 150 feet away and she hadn't seen me yet. I didn't know what the hell to do, but I know you aren't supposed to get very close to sows with young, so I immediately stood up from this hot creek and streaked for a tree that was only about ten feet away. Well, the whirlpool effect of the hot water had pumped my heart up so that I immediately blacked out, passed out, hit the tree head on like a football tackler, almost knocked myself cold, and then managed to scramble up the tree. It was the middle of October and the wind was blowing. It was cold, it was about thirty-five degrees, the wind was blowing forty miles an hour. I got up this tiny lodgepole pine tree that was only about fifteen feet high, and perched up there like a silly little bird of some kind. The grizzies sat there and ignored me totally. They didn't pay any attention, but they came within about fifty or sixty feet and ate grass for about forty-five minutes while I sat up there and froze my ass off, naked and bleeding. That was about the first time I'd seen a grizzly. Those bears made an impression.

JL   Could you describe what you do when you go out and just hang out with the griz?

DP   Uhmm. Well, the first thing that happens, especially when you're alone, is that your senses get tuned a lot quicker. A grizzly is a presence that you can take very seriously because it's the most dominant critter in the woods. It's the one chance we've got on this continent to enter an ecosystem where man is not the dominant critter. When you go into grizzly country, especially unarmed, you take a place on the food pyramid which is not at the top. Your senses and your perceptions of the world around you are necessarily altered by that, and you hear a hell of a lot better, you smell like you couldn't believe. You can train yourself to smell animals. It always happens in a very short period of time, I find. If I camp out, oh, for a week, after about day three or four, my old, rusty, dormant senses, that we probably haven't used for hundreds of years, really become alive again. That's one of the things that happens.

Having a dominant, big, powerful critter around, one who occasionally makes men his meat, instills a very powerful sense of humility, which I think is a good thing to have, because this makes you more receptive to everything around you. It opens you up. Humility is really the emotional posture behind reason. One of the very few places that I find that we can get it, in the kind of world that we're living in today, is in a really formidable, wild place. It doesn't necessarily have to have big animals, but they help.

JL You're doing a book right now. What's the name of the book, and can you describe what it's about?

DP Well, unlike people like Bill Eastlake, who come up with a title first and then write the book, I go at it the opposite way. I'm struggling through the book now, having completed a first draft, and I still haven't got a bloody title. So I don't know. It's something about bears and Vietnam. It's a bunch of what I call camping stories. They're just little trips that I took in grizzly country. And along the way, one learns a little bit about natural history. By no means is this book pretending to be authoritative or definitive or scientific. There's not going to be a footnote or a reference in the whole book. It's very much first-person narrative. I do draw some parallels with Vietnam, because Vietnam was one of the principal, or possibly even the cardinal event of my generation. And I was there. In my book, I try to tie in those relationships in two or three different ways, not overtly, necessarily.

When I came back from Vietnam I was a mess. And like I have all my life, I crawled back into the brush, which is the wilderness for me, to heal. That's one aspect of it. I really needed that kind of environment when I got back. I couldn't function around people. I had to go back into the country and rediscover the essential threads of my own humanity. So that's one thing it's about.

Another thing is that grizzly bears . . . of course, it's chauvinistic to talk about grizzly bears being endangered and threatened and going extinct, because there are plenty of them in Canada and Alaska. But what we're talking about is the bears in the lower Forty-eight. We haven't done a very good job saving grizzlies. Nobody knows how many we've got, but it's in the low hundreds. That's not much. The Yellowstone ecosystem, which is one of the two viable populations left south of Canada, probably isn't going to make it. It's certainly not going to make it genetically as the animal we've always called the grizzly. If it does survive, it's going to be selected against so heavily that it's going to be turned into some kind of black bear that looks like a grizzly.

I don't think that our bureaucracies have managed the grizzly bear very well. By and large, most of the agencies have a lousy record, even though they're doing a lot better today. In those old days, when there was a lot of mismanagement, there was a real parallel between the sort of stuff that went on in Vietnam and later in Watergate, and even on a much more mundane level that nobody cared about at the time, in and around Yellowstone when the dumps were first closed. There were a lot of bears that were killed illegally, and no one has brought that into account yet. I don't think it's terribly important because I think it belongs in the past.

The other thing that I talk about that does come from Vietnam is that I think there was something different about the war in Vietnam. It has something to do with state of moral depravity that we reached in Vietnam, that I doubt other wars saw as commonly among such a broad spectrum of troops. Part of that is reflected by the total bankruptcy of a thing like the body count, which is the only way we had to tell if we were winning over there. That leads to a series of propositions, none of which is very pleasant. I think it's no accident we ended up with My Lai's. We had a lot of little My Lai's over there. That affected the people who were there, and our nation.

The way we treat other human beings, especially of other cultures, people who speak different languages and who are of other races, comes from how we've evolved in terms of seeing otherness. Largely that comes from the natural world. In our evolution as a species and as a civilization, it's our relationship to wild animals. It's always been a history of seeing them as extensions of ourselves, as kin, as things that are different from us but related to us. I think that's something we're losing today. One of the few places that we can get it is in that wild country that's going away so soon, with those big animals that are so expendable, that are hard to justify these days in a world where poverty's everywhere and starvation is not uncommon. That's why I'm fighting to keep part of this around. I think it is a way for human beings to heal themselves collectively.

JL   That brings something up that I've thought about a lot. Do you have any sense of the animistic or mythic when you relate to the grizzly bear?

DP   I have my own little private ceremonies. When my culture doesn't provide ceremonies, I just bloody make up my own. A lot of my book deals with my own little ceremonies. The first chapter is simply the story of taking a grizzly bear skull back to the cave where she hibernated. And the last chapter is a pilgrimage out to the desert to visit a special cairn, which is essentially a monument to my own dead. But, in between the first and last chapter, I've tried to enumerate the ceremonial and ritualistic relationships of men and bears, which actually starts 100,000 years ago, with Neanderthal man in those caves in Switzerland and Germany, which is usually referred to as the Cult of the Cave Bear. What that represents is the birth of religion among the ancestors of our species. It turns out that the bear probably was the original model for spiritual renewal. He goes into a deathlike state in the wintertime. He goes underground and emerges in the spring, with new life sometimes, with new cubs. Some of the first burials of human bones were accompanied by bear bones, both brown bear and cave bear, in Europe. From the earliest ethnographic records, there's a whole circumpolar cult of the master bear, which is just pervasive as hell everywhere in the northern hemisphere. It's in the Scandinavian countries, and you find it all across Europe, Siberia, northern Japan, British Columbia, and Labrador. Usually brown bear, but all kinds of bears are there, and I just try to point this out.

The American Indians had a rich tradition of relationships with animals, of which the bear is probably the clearest example. For instance, on this continent, where there are no primates, the animal which most closely resembles man is the bear. The bear stands upright. It's an omnivore, the only very big omnivore like ourselves. And it's very humanlike in a lot of its gestures, the way it uses its paw, its diet; it snores when it sleeps; it cuffs its kids when they mess up . . . lots of little things. I just try to bring out the richness of tradition which our culture has mostly left behind, back in our tribal origins somewhere in Europe. It's not that far away, you know. You can still see throughout the world today that really rich, ritualistic ceremonial tradition of men and women with animals.

JL   I talked to a friend the other day who said that he thought this is the age when traditional man will probably become extinct. I asked him if he thought there was any way we could tap into what traditional man knows to see if we could resurrect something that I think may have begun to atrophy. Do you think that there's any chance that we can resurrect some of those values, or at least evolve new values that may tap into the old ones and keep us sane?

DP   Well, I'm an optimist, of course. I see our survival as so collective these days that I don't think we have any alternative. If we can't find the grace to allow those last few bears space enough on this planet to live alongside us, I certainly think we're not going to find the fundamental humanity and the restraint to keep from pulling the rip cords on each other and blowing the whole place to smithereens. So I think the only chance we've got is to try to realize that our little hunk of Western culture may not make it without some infusion of elements that we can still find in other cultures and other traditions—a way of relating to the natural world, which is one of humility and reverence for life, and tolerance. There are lots of ways to learn that, and a lot of native people have a richness of spiritual life that we really are lacking today. I think that's a great place to look. The original model for all that is the natural world, and I think we've got to keep hunks of it around for our own salvation.

JL Yeah, they're predicting that we'll be up around eight billion by 2020.

DP Which no one can argue with. Of course, population is as important as anything else, and nuclear war is important. I've just sort of arbitrarily chosen to fight for a little bit of wild country. But what I see behind it all is if big wild animals can be anything for free men and women, they can be real symbols of resistance, of stubbornness. They are recalcitrant, indomitable critters, and that's what we need these days. We need a little bit of that spunk. I think we've got to resist.

DAVE FOREMAN

I FIRST MET DAVE FOREMAN in a telephone conversation in 1971, when Dave was the New Mexico lobbyist for the Wilderness Society and I was working with an eco-anarchist non-organization called the Black Mesa Defense Fund. Dave and I were bemoaning the insidious onslaught of mineral extractors and land developers (who have subsequently done a hell of a job ruining much of the mythic landscape of the American Southwest).

Dave has remained in the forefront of the environmental battle. Some time ago, Dave realized that environmental organizations tended to result in the cloning of the bureaucratic state of mind, and that if he were to be a successful environmentalist, he would have to leave the bureaucracy and proceed unfettered. Dave and a few other unfettered individuals formed Earth First!, a composite of loosely affiliated people who understand with great clarity that our biosphere is in grave jeopardy because of our overabundant presence on the planet, and that there is absolutely nothing more important than this lethal and mind-numbing fact. Dave Foreman and other Earth First!-ers are dedicated to non-violent, direct action to protect the planet from human

*greed, human thoughtlessness and human law. There are few
for whom I personally have greater respect than Dave
Foreman.*

JACK LOEFFLER   Could you please tell me how you began with
Earth First! in the first place?

DAVE FOREMAN   Well, I had worked for eight years for the Wilderness Society, as their Southwest rep in New Mexico and Arizona, and then as their chief lobbyist and issues coordinator in
Washington, D.C. I was there during the time of the Carter administration. I basically came to the conclusion that we were being
co-opted by the establishment, that having influence and all made
us more moderate. We compromised more, thought about prag-
matic politics instead of biocentric ethics. And so with several
other people who had worked for the Friends of the Earth or the
Wilderness Society, or who were active Sierra Club members,
we decided that the time had come for an environmental group
that wouldn't compromise, that would base itself on ethics
instead of pragmatics, and that would take strong action to try
to stop the destruction of the wilderness.

JL   Could you describe some of the techniques that you employ,
with regard to protecting the wilderness?

DF   We've been active primarily on this in the Oregon National
Forest. We have taken nonviolent direct action as developed by
Gandhi and Martin Luther King and the antinuclear movement
and adapted it to wilderness preservation. There are certain
changes in it. We've had people go in and stand in front of bulldozers constructing logging roads into wild areas. We've had people sit in dynamite-loaded fields to stop mountains from being
blown away. We've hugged trees to keep trees from being cut down
by chain saws . . . a whole variety of things like that. We've
blocked logging trucks. In the last two summers, we've had over

100 people arrested in Oregon in some twenty separate incidents. And we've been doing some of the same thing in Northern California to save old growth redwoods, as well.

JL   How big an area do you conceive of as your territory?

DF   The whole world. We're Earth First! And we're in close contact with Australian conservationists who have pioneered the use of nonviolent direct action for the preservation of wilderness. These people have stopped the Franklin River Dam in Tasmania, stopped rain forest logging in New South Wales, and have been working for the last couple of years in northern Queensland to stop the eroding and destruction of the Daintree Rain Forest. We've been in communication with the natives of the Solomon Islands, who have used a little stronger direct action fighting Unilever and other international logging companies. And we're in touch with the Indians in British Columbia right now, who are prepared to engage in nonviolent direct action to stop the logging of Mere's Island off Vancouver Island. So our network is spreading out all over the world.

JL   Do you have any idea how many members Earth First! has?

DF   Well, it's hard to say, since we really don't have a membership list. One of the things we decided when we started Earth First! is that when you take on the organization structure of the corporate state you also tend to take on its ideology, and that if we were going to stay true to our biocentric principles, the only organization structure to emulate would be the hunter-gatherer tribe, which means no formal leadership, no hierarchy, and no formal membership. So, I edit the Earth First! newspaper, and people subscribe to that, but how many people consider themselves Earth Firsters is hard to say. Probably somewhere around 10,000 in the United States.

JL   That's very impressive.

DF   And those people are engaged at all levels, from the 500 or so people in Oregon and Northern California, who in one way or another are involved in direct action, to folks who are Sierra

Club chapter chairpersons and lobbyists for other groups who are at heart Earth First!-ers but are still working in the system and trying to get their groups to take a stronger stand.

JL   It must cost a fair amount of money to keep Earth First! afloat. How do you solicit funding?

DF   We wanted to get away from the endless cycle of sending out fundraising letters. It seems like the Sierra Club and Wilderness Society and other groups spend about eighty percent of the money they get from fundraising on fundraising. We want to see all of our money go to best use. So even though there is an Earth First! Foundation, a separate entity which does try to raise money and then give grants out, the primary way we have raised money is subscriptions to our newspaper and the sales of T-shirts, bumper stickers, "Heyduke Lives" patches and calendars. Then we try to channel that money back in to the movement. We want to give people something very direct for their money, and not be in the position of asking for too many contributions. We do separate the different elements of the movement financially, so that the Oregon Earth First! group has its own bank account, and we run solicitations for them in our newspaper. People can send contributions directly to them, so the money doesn't go for overhead and administration. It goes right for the action. Nobody in Earth First! gets a salary since we aren't set up as an organization. The money goes where the action is.

JL   That's very commendable. Can you isolate some areas, say in the Southwest, that really need some sort of attention by either Earth First!-ers or people of like spirit?

DF   Well, there are several areas. One that we have been paying a lot of attention to is Canyon Lands nuclear dump. We've been watching that very closely for several years and laying the groundwork for nonviolent direct action on that. Now it appears that that's one battle we may not have to fight. But we aren't positive, so we're going to continue watching. There are a number of other issues. We're very concerned about the Forest Service logging in the Santa Fe National Forest, and we are going to be talking to folks there about possible action.

Actually, our first nonviolent direct action was in New Mexico in the Bitterlake Wildlife Refuge a couple of years ago when Yates Petroleum put in an illegal road and started drilling a well illegally in the Salt Creek Wilderness. We went in and blockaded that, and eventually two of our people from Albuquerque were arrested down there.

We're looking at a lot of issues like that, and if something pops up, we're going to be involved in it. Now we're involved in other things, too. For example, we are developing wilderness proposals for BLM lands in New Mexico and Arizona. We are developing Forest Service wilderness proposals in New Mexico, with talk of a second RARE II bill in New Mexico. Our feeling is you shouldn't start with just the roadless area. You should say, "Hey, should this road not have been built?" or "Should this timber sale not have happened?" And you go in and try to build larger areas that are ecologically complete units. For example, we'd like to see the North Star Road between the Gila Wilderness and the Aldo Leopold Wilderness closed and a million-acre wilderness created down there in the Gila. And we'd like to see the reintroduction of grizzly bears and wolves, to go back to a real wilderness area instead of just a recreational park for backpackers.

JL   Ed Abbey told me that you have just finished a book, and I wonder if you could describe it.

DF   Well, the book is called *Eco Defense, a Field Guide to Monkeywrenching*. It basically comes from the frustration of having worked within the system one way or another as an environmentalist for fifteen years now, as a full-time professional environmentalist, lobbying, working through the agencies, the courts, the whole works, and finding out that it's just one big tar baby. The more you try to deal with the system, the more you get stuck in it. Eventually you realize that you aren't going to get anywhere. Yes, you're going to win little victories here and there—you're going to pick up wilderness areas that the system is willing to give you, but the dominant paradigm of our culture and the men running it, is to develop every last acre that has anything which they arrogantly call "resources" on it.

I've come to the conclusion that the most effective way to stop this industrial juggernaut is for people individually, acting in true American fashion, to go out and resist it. And you can resist it nonviolently, without danger to yourself or other people, and you can stop it. This includes things like spiking trees, which inhibits their commercial value for timbercutting—drive long metal nails into trees slated for logging, and those trees, when they reach the sawmill, will do extensive damage to sawmill blades. Our feeling is that there are enough people around the West spiking trees that the Forest Service and the timber companies aren't going to be interested in this marginal timber.

If you go in and properly pull up survey stakes or help erosion, wash out roads that shouldn't be there, sooner or later the Forest Service and other agencies are going to realize that they can't maintain that really expensive infrastructure of roads. A number of things like this will eventually cause the retreat of industrial civilization from millions of acres. In effect, we can create our own *de facto* wilderness and cause civilization to stay away. I visualize this as simple self-defense of the wilderness. We aren't subversive, we aren't trying to overthrow any system. We're just saying "Hands off, don't come into these wild areas, leave them alone. We're the grizzly, we're the wolf, we're the spotted owl, we're the ponderosa pine, we're the creosote bush, practicing self-defense." And it's nonviolent self-defense. In the book, we go out of our way to stress safety measures, how not to hurt people, how not to put yourself in danger. How not to get captured by the police, for example.

JL   I've been developing the notion of a geriatric kamikaze unit.

DF   Right! Yes! I always think if I get an incurable disease, I will make good use of it.

JL   At this moment in time, can you foresee how your role in the future is going to evolve?

DF   It's hard to tell. I don't think any of us can predict the future. I have some strange ideas about the future. I do not see any way possible for the current trend to keep going. Sooner or later, things are going to have to crash. I think we're in a car going ninety miles an hour down a dead-end street with a brick wall right in front of us. We're trying to look for the brakes, and I don't think there are any. I think we're in a classic biological curve of exploding population, exploding toxic production, exploding destruction of the earth, and the only way that type of population curve ends is with a dramatic drop-off.

I sometimes tell people that I think the Earth has sort of evolved some of us—if you look at the human race not as the consciousness of the earth, but as the cancer of the earth—that we're a disease ecologically, and that maybe Nature has evolved some of us as antibodies. That's the only way I can explain why some of us love wilderness and other people have no conception of it at all. And so, our role in the future, I think, is to try to preserve as many areas of natural diversity as possible. To make sure that there are some wolves and grizzlies, ponderosa pines and spotted owls, snail darters and what have you, so that when this human insanity runs its course, there is life to come back and repopulate the world. And hopefully also to develop the ethics and the potential for a human society that can live in harmony with the rest of the planet after this industrial madness burns itself out. Those are really the two things I'm trying to do in the long term. One is to lay the groundwork for a human society in the future that is ecologically based, and the other is to preserve as much natural diversity now as we can.

JL   Beautiful. Has any of your thinking been influenced by the mores of indigenous peoples like the Hopis, or . . .

DF   Yes, it has. What we try to do is go back to the hunter-gatherers. I think if you look at the current resurge, if you read Paul Shepard, if you read other thinkers on this, you can see that we have really a twisted view of what hunter-gatherer life was like. In reality it was the best life people have ever lived. I think we have to try to get back to that. Somewhere along with the development of agriculture we made a really bad mistake. Like Gary Snyder says, "We've been caught in a back eddy in the stream of human life for the last 10,000 years." Somehow we've got to get out of that back eddy and re-enter the main stream, which is primitive culture, if you want to call it that, organic culture. When we talk about deep ecology, the attitude of biocentrism, we say it's the newest philosophy in the world, but it's also the oldest philosophy in the world. If you could go back to an American Indian of several thousand years ago, or to a Neanderthal, or to a bushman in the Kalahari desert, or to an Australian aborigine, and talk to them about philosophy, they would find the philosophy of Western civilization or Eastern civilization right now totally mind-boggling and arrogant and insane. How could we consider ourselves so apart from and superior to life on the rest of the planet? How could we conceive that we somehow have *carte blanche* to dominate and destroy? If you could go back and talk to paleo-Indians who lived with the dire wolf, the smilodon (saber-toothed tiger), the cave bear, the mastodons, the wooly rhinos and the giant ground sloth, they would have been astounded at the attitude that human beings are in charge of the planet. They had an attitude that all these creatures are equal, and have an equal right to be here. And that's what we're saying philosophically. Everything has intrinsic value. You don't preserve wilderness because you like to hike in it or because it is pretty to look at. You preserve wilderness because wilderness has a right to exist for its own sake. The grizzly bear has just as much right to her own life as any one of us has to ours. And if you want to take it even further, it says that a species of mosquito is just as important as the human species is—that what's really important is not the individual or the species, but the community, the interlocking collection of different life forms and what we call inanimate objects that make up a community in a stable, diverse, healthy ecosystem. That's really where evolution takes place, that's really where the life force is. You can't separate any of it. That's what's worth preserving. Not individuals, or species, but the community.

JL   Even though our species may have condemned itself to some sort of oblivion, do you think that biota, as we understand it, has a chance of succeeding?

DF   I think so. I think that no matter what we do, there's going to be something left around, even if it's cockroaches. Who knows what will come back in a billion years or so? I sort of like what Russell Means of AIM had to say once. He said that the Earth has been abused, the powers have been abused, that the Earth is striking back. If I've got any optimism left in me after being battered around by the political system for the last fifteen years, it is that there is some basic intelligence inherent in the whole body of Earth and that she is going to do something to clean up the mess that we're making.

GARY DEWALT

*In the 16th century, by Christian reckoning, the castle
town of Hiroshima was founded near the southern end of the
Island of Honshu, Japan. Some four centuries later,
Hiroshima gained the apocalyptic distinction of being the .
first city to be destroyed by an atomic bomb. Some 75,000
human beings were either killed or fatally injured. Many
consider the bombing of Hiroshima to have been a military
necessity to bring to an end a war that forever changed the
face of the globe. Others regard the atomic bombing of
Hiroshima as perhaps humanity's greatest moment of infamy.
Be that as it may, the shroud that surrounded the bombing of
Hiroshima hid many secrets in its fold.*

*One secret that has come to light is the fact that a crew of
American Army Air Corpsmen were being held in captivity
at Hiroshima at the time of the bombing. Gary Dewalt, a
film-maker from Santa Fe, New Mexico, completed a
documentary film concerning this crew. I asked him to
describe the genesis and evolution of the idea that was to
result in the film.*

GARY DEWALT   Well, the title of the film is *Genbaku Shi,* which in Japanese, when it's translated into English, means "killed by the atomic bomb." And the idea for the film arose in early 1980. I had an interest in making a film that related to the use of nuclear weapons. I had been influenced somewhat by reading Robert Lifton's book called *Death and Life,* which is a study of the survivors of Hiroshima. I was so struck by the devastation which the bomb delivered, and its physical as well as social and psychological results, that I became interested in making a film about the use of nuclear weapons.

I approached Dr. Barton Bernstein, who's a historian at Stanford University and a specialist on the Truman Administration and the Cold War. Dr. Bernstein, in passing, said, "By the way, do you know about the American prisoners of war who were killed by the atomic bomb?" I told him that it was the first time I had ever heard that story. He pulled out a small file, and said, "If you'd like, take this to your hotel and look it over this evening and see what you think."

So I took the file that Dr. Bernstein had given me back to my hotel and as I looked through it, the file had the essence of the story. In the early 1970s a researcher at an institute connected with Hiroshima University had discovered in some historical archives a list of Americans who had been killed. This list was then published in Japan and in turn was picked up by some American scholars, including Dr. Bernstein, who started to pursue the case in the United States.

I became intrigued by the story because it appeared, upon a cursory examination of Bernstein's documents, that the United States government had been less than forthcoming as far as notifying members of the families was concerned. Also they were claiming that concise statements about who was in Hiroshima, who was killed, who was not killed, could not be made because records had been destroyed in a military archive fire in St. Louis in, I believe, 1973.

I took the file back to Bernstein the next morning, told him that I was very intrigued by this story, and if he would agree to cooperate with me I would like to resume the search where he had left off a couple of years earlier, with the hope that the end result would be a documentary film about American POWs killed by the bomb.

After I returned to Santa Fe, there followed a period of about six months where I retraced Dr. Bernstein's steps and was given the same response by the military—that is, the documents that were necessary for looking more closely at the statements made by the Japanese that a number of Americans had been killed, simply were not available because they'd been destroyed in a fire in St. Louis in 1973. But I continued to ask. I tried to think of where there might be some documentation. It occurred to me that the Veterans Administration might have something.

Finally, I connected with a woman there who was a career employee, had worked for the Veterans Administration since the end of World War II. She took me aside one day and said, "What you should know is that the files that you want, the files that will allow you to make some definitive statement, indeed do exist, and they exist in the office of the Adjutant General, and they are what are known as '293 files.' These are files that were created when someone was either declared missing in action or killed in action during World War II."

I must say I was quite surprised, because I had been told by the Adjutant General's office that there really were no documents that would allow anyone to make a definitive statement. So, with the information from the Veterans Administration, I returned to Santa Fe, and filed a series of Freedom of Information Act requests addressed to the Adjutant General's office, saying that I was aware that these files did exist, and could I please see the "293 files" of two or three individuals whose names I had extracted from the Japanese list. At this point it was purely a test to see if such documents did exist.

There followed, within a matter of weeks after my inquiry, a manila envelope which contained these "293 files." And indeed, they did confirm very clearly that there had been Americans at Hiroshima, that the American military was aware of the deaths. I must say it was a great surprise, because all along the other researchers, including myself in the very early stages, had been told that such files did not exist.

With that response, I began then to file Freedom of Information Act requests on additional names as I would pull them from the Japanese records. One by one the files came in, confirming in substance and in detail the content of the Japanese documents. Over a period of approximately eight to nine months, we were able to solidly identify ten individual prisoners of war who were at Hiroshima at the time the bomb was dropped. So as we compared and contrasted the Japanese and American documents, we were able to come up with what we thought was a very solid list.

But it left a lot of unanswered questions. Where were the Americans housed? Were they in Hiroshima? Did all of them die at the time of the blast? Did some of them survive? What happened to their guards? With those questions remaining, we decided that a trip to Japan would be necessary.

We secured a very small grant, which allowed us in the summer of 1983 to travel to Japan where we began interviewing former members of the Japanese military, people who had been guards, people who had been translators. And we were able to fill in a lot of the missing information, a lot of the gaps that existed between the Japanese and the American documents.

AUTHOR'S NOTE I was fortunate to be a member of the film crew that travelled with Gary Dewalt to Japan. Jack Parsons was the cinematographer, and I recorded the sound. In Hiroshima, on August 6, 1983, we attended the ceremony commemorating the thirty-eighth anniversary of the dropping of the atomic bomb. We encountered pilgrims from all over the world. There were thousands of us passing through Peace Memorial Park, an area near the center of the atomic blast—an area that has been set aside for all time, wherein one may contemplate the consequences of nuclear war. I was able to record the sounds of many who created their own music on behalf of peace. I recorded the great bell, which was specially cast to be hung in Peace Memorial Park. Any who so wish can toll that haunting bell, in the hope that sanity and peace will prevail. In closing, I asked Dewalt what hopes he has with regard to the effect of his film, *Genbaku Shi*, on the American public.

GD   A point that Robert Lifton has consistently made since he began his research, I think now more than twenty years ago, into the psychological and social impact of the use of nuclear weapons is that the destructive power of the weapons is so great, the ability to annihilate within seconds large populations, is so fantastic, so horrific that a lot of people go into a state which Lifton describes as psychological numbing. In other words, it's so difficult, so traumatic to comprehend, you put a distance between that reality and your own personal being. He consistently makes the point that it's extremely difficult to get people to look closely at the impact of nuclear weapons and the kind of devastation and human destruction that they bring. You have to take it down to very, very small cases. We're not talking about statistics. We're not talking about body counts. We're actually talking about single individuals, human beings, that add up to those horrific numbers. These are people who would be musicians, who would be doctors, taxicab drivers, mechanics. It's the loss of human potential that we're talking about, not statistics and numbers. I happen to agree with Dr. Lifton on that count, and I think it's important that when we talk about the destructive power of nuclear weapons and the indiscriminate disaster that they bring on human populations that we have to look at who gets killed where nuclear weapons are being used.

These Americans who were killed—Americans who had plans to return, to be farmers, auto mechanics, college professors—because they happened to be in the wrong place at the wrong time and suffered the indiscriminate nature of nuclear weapons, were extinguished. Their futures are forever gone. My hope is that by focusing on these individual lives, we will come to understand the loss of human potential, the indiscriminate destructive power of these weapons. They're more than tools of warfare. Because of their indiscriminate nature, they are eradicators of human experience and human potential. The important point is nuclear weapons are totally indiscriminate.

PHILIP WHALEN

IN THE LATTER HALF of the 1950s, I was a young jazz musician
serving my time in the 433rd Army Band in the Mojave Desert.
In the summer of '57, we were transported to Desert Rock at
the Nevada Proving Grounds. On occasion, we would don our
Frank Buck garb, assume military formation and stand in
pre-dawn Nevada performing marches that were regarded as
militarily invigorating. Suddenly the bomb would go off in a
maelstrom of indescribable colors and then the mushroom
cloud would stretch skyward like a giant radioactive dildo.

I performed three bombsworth before the Army
relinquished me to the streets, my horn in my hand, my mind
thoroughly blown, unstuck from mainstream American
values but definitely not unhinged. I gravitated
northwestward to San Francisco and Marin County where I
encountered people who were searching for new paths through
the culturescape of America. Poetry and jazz were superb
vehicles of expression in those days when the counterculture
energized and a new intellectual milieu became apparent.

One of America's great poets, Philip Whalen, was in the
vanguard of his artform. He, Gary Snyder and Lew Welch had
been roommates at Reed College. Philip has written
prodigiously and has become a Zen monk respected and

admired by all who read him and beloved by all who know him. He has authored two novels and several books of poetry, including On Bear's Head *and* Heavy Breathing. *He is featured reading his poetry on an album entitled* By and Large. *One time I asked Philip to describe to me the genesis of one of the great literary events in American history.*

————

PHILIP WHALEN   Well, Beat Generation, at this point we have to get very careful and historically accurate and whatnot, and repeat what's in all the textbooks, which is true—that that name was invented by Kerouac to deal with a period in New York after the war, say about 1947. John Clellon Holmes, a friend of Jack's who has written several novels, had an assignment to write an article for the *New York Times Book Review,* or some other New York paper, about current American novel writing. So here was this new generation.

They used to say that there was a Lost Generation after the First World War; what could we call where we're at after the Second World War? Jack said, "Well, why don't you call it the 'Beat Generation,' because we're all beat. We're all tired of the war and we don't have any money. Nobody knows who we are. We're just sort of out of everything and we're kind of way out on a fringe somewhere and kind of moping along. So why don't you say Beat Generation." So that's where that came from. It dealt, to some degree, with life around the drug scene and high mopery scene around Times Square in 1947, which involved Burroughs and Corso and Ginsberg and Kerouac and a number of other people. Sheri Martinelli, the painter, was around on the edges there somewhere. Various other people who were later celebrated were in and around that trip.

I guess it was 1954 that Ginsberg came out to San Francisco and hung around and got a job as some sort of market researcher. He was running around in a business suit and a necktie and white shirt, doing whatever a market researcher does. At one point he went to see Kenneth Rexroth, and said, in his usual way, "What's happening around here?" And Rexroth said, "Well, nothing's happening to speak of." And he said, "Why don't you make something happen, why don't you do something yourself?" And Allen said, "Well, what'll I do?" And Rexroth said, "Hire a hall and get your friends together and have a poetry reading." So Allen thought, "Well that's a funny and marvelous idea, who should I get hold of?" And Rexroth said, "Well Philip Lamantia is in town, and in Berkeley there's a funny youngster called Gary Snyder who knows people, and Mike McClure is a young guy who is around here. You ought to find him." So Allen said, "Oh, great."

Snyder says that one day this gentlemen with a business suit and a necktie and white shirt showed up at this little shack he was living in at Berkeley and introduced himself, and said, "Here I am. I'm Allen Ginsberg. Rexroth told me to come and see you and talk about doing a poetry reading." So Gary said, "Oh, okay."

I was working on the Sourdough Mountain Lookout in Washington State at that time, and he wrote to me and said, "As soon as you get down, you must come to Berkeley and get situated, and then we're going to have this poetry reading in October in San Francisco. This guy Allen Ginsberg has organized this funny thing and we want you to be in it." So I wrote back, "Okay, I'll see you when I get there." But the fire season ran until the middle of September that year. Anyway I got to California before October got started, and presently this first big poetry bash happened on October 6, 1955.

Now then, books disagree about his, but there are various letters and other things around whereby it can be easily proved that this was done in 1955, because Ginsberg, in the summer of '55 or in the fall of '55 when I first met him, was busy cutting and polishing the version of "Howl" that he read that evening, and having a lot of fun doing it. So this reading was an unexpected excitement. Suddenly there were maybe two hundred fifty people in a very small space, who had heard about it some way or another. I had helped Allen address a whole bunch of postcards announcing the thing. Then we sent it out to the mailing list that belonged to the Six Gallery where we read. All these people showed up and were very excited about what was happening, that something was going on new and exciting. Of course, this was the first time any heard the "Howl" poem, and that just knocked everybody cuckoo. I think Ferlinghetti was present, and at that moment he waltzed up to Ginsberg and said, "I want to publish that thing. Give it to me."

The next thing that happened, of course, was that Rexroth was very happy, and he went to Ruth Witt Diamant, who was running the poetry center at San Francisco State, and said, "Listen, you ought to get these guys to read on your program, because they're all doing funny things that are new and exciting and so forth." Of course at that time, her program was very, very straight. She was producing Dylan Thomas and Wystan Auden. All of the great American academic poets were coming on her series at the college, and it was always very fancy and very elegant and marvelous and expensive.

Well, anyway, she took him up on it. She simply invited all of us to come on different weeks and read at the Telegraph Hill Neighborhood Center under the sponsorship of the Poetry Center. They advertised it and whatnot, and these evenings were very successful. McClure read and Ginsberg read and Gary read and I read and I forget who all else, but in any case, those were the first public trips that we made.

Then in the following spring in Berkeley, a friend of Gary who belonged to a little theater group arranged with her to borrow their theater one Sunday, and a whole bunch of us read on that occasion, a whole lot of people that have dropped out of sight since then. But there was a very large audience, and everybody was totally happy and gaga about the whole thing.

I think it was, say, '56 or early '57 that Donald Allen appeared from New York. He was then editing the *Evergreen Review*, which had just started publication from Grove Press. He came out and just got hold of everybody and said, "Please give me poems. I'm going to do a San Francisco issue of the *Evergreen Review*." Harry Radel, the photographer, showed up and took pictures of everybody, and then Donald printed poems from all of us. That second issue of the *Evergreen Review* was quite an interesting one, what with a chunk of "Howl" and some McClure and Ferlinghetti and Gary and me. From then on, all of those who had become most known and most famous, like Allen and Jack and Gregory, were very, very generous about telling people who asked them for work, "You should ask Snyder and you should ask Whalen and ask various other people—McClure and so on—to please send poems; you ought to pick up on them, because they're doing funny things, too." And so with the help of Corso and Ginsberg and Kerouac, our stuff got to be better known, which was very happy.

INTERLUDE AT L.A. AIRPORT

ONE DAY IN THE LATE SPRING of 1972, my wife Katherine and I arrived at Third Mesa to pick up four friends, including David Monongye and Thomas Banyacya. We were all on our way to Los Angeles to board a plane which would take us to Stockholm, Sweden, where we were to attend the U.N. Conference on the Human Environment. Unbeknownst to Kath and me, the four Hopis had refused to acquire U.S. passports on the grounds that they were citizens of the Hopi Independent Nation, not the United States of America.

Through the next twenty-four hours, Kath and I scrounged old parchment looking paper, beautiful hand-tanned buckskin, four eagle prayer feathers and a typewriter. With these we fashioned four handcrafted documents. Each of these documents bore the name of one of the Hopis, a real or hypothetical birthdate (David Monongye was so old that his true birthdate had yet to be revealed), and the inscription: "The bearer of this passport is a citizen of the Hopi Independent Nation. This passport is valid as long as the Sun shines, the Grass grows, and the Water flows." Each of these passports was appropriately signed and then blessed with corn pollen administered by David Monongye.

Walpi, First Mesa — Hopi Village, 1932

We all piled into my truck and drove west from Third Mesa while David sang Hopi songs, accompanying himself by rattling a plastic jar filled with vitamin C tablets.

The great day came and many of us were gathered in the lobby of the L.A. International Airport. I walked up to the TWA ticket counter with six airline tickets and six passports, two of which indicated that the bearers were U.S. citizens. The counter human regarded the handful of paper, leather and feathers. The cast of her official countenance had somehow slipped, slowly to be replaced by a strange expression I was unable to identify. Finally, she placed the documents on the counter and brushed off her hands while corn pollen delicately altered the hue of her uniform. She looked at me very keenly and said, "This is a joke."

"I beg your pardon," I replied.

"These aren't real passports," she said, indicating our handiwork.

"Oh, yes," I said. "These are Hopi passports."

"There is no such thing as a Hopi passport."

"There certainly is. You can see for yourself that there are four Hopi passports right there in front of you."

"These are not legal passports," said the counter human, her face flushing.

"They're certainly as legal as those two green ones, there," said I, beginning to feel somewhat defensive.

"You can't be serious. Hopi Indians are American citizens just like any other American citizens. They can't have Hopi passports because Hopi passports are not recognized as legal by the United States Government." She was getting angry.

"Look," I said, trying to be a reasonable fellow, "the Hopis regard themselves as members of the Hopi Independent Nation which is at least six or seven hundred years older than the United States of America. It's OK if the United States wants to think of the Hopis as U.S. citizens. They can think anything they want. But the Hopis don't think of themselves as anything but Hopis. That's the key here. Therefore, they prefer having their own passports."

"Only U.S. passports are legal. Hopi passports are against the law!"

"The only law that has meaning is natural law. The Hopis regard the United States as unnatural!"

"I don't want to talk to you any more. I'm getting my supervisor." She left. And so did the TWA flight to Stockholm. With everybody but the Hopis and Kath and me.

The day wore on and I wore thin on everybody's nerves. Two officious men on the government dole claiming to be employed by the U.S. State Department had tried to intervene with the usual blather about this law and that, modified by article number such and so, clarified by sub-paragraph F.U., etc.

Finally, a nordic-looking gent in a black uniform with gold bars and stars whom I had noticed observing for the last couple of hours and who gave the appearance of having enjoyed the whole ludicrous situation, came over to me, interrupted the agents and said sedately, "I'm the pilot of Scandinavian Airlines Flight 711 and I'd be delighted to take you all on my plane to Stockholm."

And so four Hopis, carrying their kits, Kath carrying hers, and I bringing up the rear with my kit crammed full of cans of green chile walked single file past the flustered feds to the awaiting plane. I looked back over my shoulder at the bedraggled bureaucrats and honored them with my deadliest grin.

We got to Stockholm and the Swedes stamped the Hopi passports, as did the Danes at a later date. And in spite of the State Department who threatened to ban the Hopis' re-entry, everyone made it home to the protection of their local deities. *Support your local deity!!*

GARY SNYDER

WHILE WE WERE ATTENDING the U.N. Conference on the Human Environment in Stockholm, it came to pass that Kath and I briefly shared our pad with poet Gary Snyder. We were loosely affiliated with a larger group of eco-activists who had assembled there to demonstrate concern for the health of the planet. After the conference had ended and most of the participants had departed, Gary, Kath and I remained and comprised a clean-up squad to ensure that we left our collective camp, a gallery on Pilgaten, as we had found it. An enormous amount of paper had been generated—pamphlets, magazines, fliers—all transported from the U.S. to Stockholm. There it sat in the aftermath, unread, unnecessary, unwanted, and we three knew we had to deal with it. We hired a trailer, loaded it to capacity and then hauled it to the city dump where we deposited this collective environmental message to the world.

Over the years, Gary Snyder and I have remained friends in spite of distance and busy-ness. Not long ago, it was my karma to transport a beautiful 19th century bronze Burmese Buddha from a zendo in New Mexico to a zendo near Gary's home in northern California. One July morn, Philip Whalen and I placed the two-foot-high Buddha in the passenger seat of my pickup truck, strapped it in with the seat belt and bid farewell. The Buddha and I slowly meandered through many of my old and sacred haunts in the southwestern quadrant of the United States. We visited the San Juan River, Navajo Mountain, Capitol Reef, some secret places, Pyramid Lake. Finally we arrived at Gary's home. Gary and I carried the Buddha to its destination, and commenced a conversation that lasted well into the night. We spoke of many things, including the Beat generation, the hippie scene of the 1960s and the environmentalists and eco-anarchists who emerged in the late 1960s, a scene that fortunately remains with us today. Gary ruminated on his literary forebears. Gary Snyder is one of the great poets of our time, with many books to his credit, including Riprap, The Back Country, Regarding Wave. *And* Turtle Island, *for which he won the Pulitzer Prize. He is also one of America's great environmental philosophers and, to my mind, a fine anarchist.*

———

JACK LOEFFLER   You're one of the truly distinguished men of letters in America, and one of the characteristics that really does distinguish you, over and above the fact of your writing, is your high regard for the natural world and the role of traditional people in the natural world. Could you tell me when you first realized this concern?

GARY SNYDER   I can't remember when I didn't have it. Thinking back, I just grew up with it, I guess, living in the country—rural Washington State north of Seattle on a dairy farm, with second and third growth timberland gradually coming back. There were great ten-to-twelve-foot-high stumps left from the original logging of the cedar and the Douglas fir, with springboard notches chopped in the stump way up toward the top. I put a lot together from talking with older people, hearing the stories. I wouldn't have phrased it this way at that time, but I grew up with thoughts of what natural ecosystems are, and what a disturbed ecosystem is, and about the puzzle, "How do human beings fit their ways of life into the natural world?" Seeing what took place in the state of Washington through the '30s, I intuitively arrived at a concern for all of that. Fishing and forestry.

JL   You've spent a fair amount of time with people who are regarded as indigenous. There seems to be a real difference in points of view between indigenous people and the dominant culture of the 20th century. Would you talk about some of those differences?

GS   I'm still learning and thinking about what those differences are. What does indigenous mean? What does aboriginal mean? What does native mean? The only people who might have difficulty understanding the layers of implications of being native to a place are people such as ourselves, transplanted Euro-Americans, whether in North America or in Australia. South America is another case, slightly different. At any rate, transplanted 20th century Euro-Americans are totally focused on their own social, political and economic networks that are spread widely and draw economically from sources all over the world. Most people are far removed from any direct production. Few people are involved with the first level of production, and the first level of production is plants—photosynthesis. Those who are involved with it, so-called farmers, are removed from it by their intensive use of fertilizers, pesticides, herbicides, equipment, piped-in water and professional university farm advisors. The tools and the information by which people all over the globe have for millennia known how to do what they did, is unavailable to them. They don't even know it exists.

Indigenous or aboriginal or native, first of all, has to be understood as the natural state of affairs—as is the amount of sunlight falling on the Earth, spread in varying degrees. Following from that, plants and their communities form mosaics of type and structure appropriate to the nature and degree of solar energy falling on that spot. The economic systems of various cultures are precisely adapted to that area—to the plants that grow in that area. Indigeneity is having the plant and animal, soil and water knowledges that are specific to those mosaics. And in turn, the sense of spirit, the sense of sacredness, the cultural devices, and the songs and dances flow in terms of that as well. All of that is normal, and all of that is obviously sustainable. It's what sustainability is. Imagine it as a mosaic of countless thousands of relatively small watershed or plant communities, or soil-type bioregions to which a variety of cultures are flexibly adapted. It's not deterministic, though. Arctic peoples of Siberia have different manners of style than Arctic peoples of North America, so this is not environmental determinism. The closer you get to the subsistence base, the more deterministic it is. The song and dance has a lot of flexibility.

JL   In our culture, or in our country, we have a lot of different places that I would regard as bioregions, and there is a certain ethnicity that prevails in many of them. I recall a conversation we had a long time ago, where you were talking about decentralization, and revivifying an agrarian point of view. Subsequent to that conversation, the term bioregionalism seems to have evolved. Could you define bioregionalism, or the context in which you think of it?

GS   Well, I can try, I suppose, as well as the next person. It's not in the dictionary, but it is being used, and it's being recognized even by professional geographers now as a term that has come into some kind of currency. So "bioregion," the term itself, would refer to a region that is defined in some way by its plant and animal characteristics, its life zone characteristics that flow from soil and climate—the territory of Douglas fir, or the region of coastal redwoods; short grass prairie, medium grass prairie and tall grass prairie; high desert and low desert. Those could be, or verge on, bioregional definitions. When you get it more specific, you might say Northern Plains short grass prairie, upper Missouri watershed, or some specific watershed of the upper Missouri. The criteria are flexible, but even though the boundaries and the delineations can vary according to your criteria, there is roughly something we all agree on. Just like we all agree on what a given language is, even though languages are fluid in their dialects. So bioregionalism is a kind of creative branch of the environmental movement that strives to re-achieve indigeneity, re-achieve aboriginality, by learning about the place and what really goes on there.

Bioregionalism goes beyond simple geography or biology by its cultural concern, its human concern. It is to know not only the plants and animals of a place, but also the cultural information of how people live there—the ones who know how to do it. Knowing the deeper mythic, spiritual, archetypal implications of a fir, or a coyote, or a bluejay might be to know from both inside and outside what the total implications of a place are. So it becomes a study not only of place, but a study of psyche in place. That's what makes it so interesting. In a way, it seems to me, that it's the first truly concrete step that has been taken since Kropotkin in stating how we decentralize ourselves after the 20th century.

JL   This really interests me—your allusions to how anarchism has evolved, or co-evolved with the environmental movement within the notion of bioregionalism. An area that intrigues me, because I live there, is the Rio Grande watershed. There are Puebloans, Spaniards, and Anglos living in some sense of contiguity, yet retaining their own cultural characteristics. I shouldn't neglect to mention that the Athabaskans came in just prior to the Spanairds and resulted in the Apaches and the Navajos. So there are different cultures living in relatively peaceful coexistence. How do you conceive of different people, or people with different cultural characteristics, functioning within the bioregional context?

GS   That's a real challenge, isn't it? The first level would be the spread of hominids over the Earth, gradually, out of whatever their original home territory was, making these amazing cultural adaptations place by place, from tropic to arctic. That's the first level, the amazing flexibility of the hominids, particularly of Homo sapiens. And then the second level is comprised of the precise mosaics of adaptation that evolved, gradually, so that people learned how to make tapioca, or how to get the tannin out of acorns and make edible mush—all these wonderful skills. And the songs and dances that came out of that—that's the second level. The third level would be the maintenance of planetary internationalism via the exchange of folklore motifs, the sharing of the great mind, the deep human mind, and the continuation of trade and exchange of material objects as well as of song and dance and myth. The boundaries are always porous to those things which can be shared from mind to mind. Then the fourth level, historically, is the enlargement of migrations, raiding, and the disruptions that we witness in historical times, that are caused by waves of invading peoples pressured out by the Imperium, the forces of civilization. This process has been around about 8,000 years.

There are islands of new and old—of old people surrounded by new people. Then those people become islands surrounded by newer people. For example, the Basques became an island surrounded by Celts, probably, and then the Celts became surrounded and reduced by Romans. So the mosaics become many-layered. And a tremendous amount of human conflict and violence and ongoing struggle flows from that, such as we see in the Middle East.

Yours is a question that applies to all kinds of places over the globe. Granted that we could achieve some kind of stability in other areas—economy, politics—could multiple ethnic groups inhabiting the same region learn to live together? Well, they can in some places. In India there are large areas where the ethnicity is really extraordinary. They have worked out a *modus vivendi* with each other, which the caste system helps make possible. At any rate, my thought about it, the bioregional thought of it, is this: If people can agree to share, and agree that they all love the land—say in the Rio Grande valley—if people can first of all say, "Here we are in this place, we live here, now we are here—Navajos, Puebloans, Hispanics, Anglos, Texans, Hippies—all here together, these new diverse tribes." If we can all agree, first of all, that we're here, then the newcomers can say, "We want to treat this place as right as you learned to treat it, and we make our commitment to this place, as much as you did, and are no longer simple carpet baggers, making a fast buck to then move on." Then, even though religion, language and many other cultural things and styles might be radically different, they've got something to begin to work from, which is their shared interest in the land—their shared project of learning the land and learning what it can carry, learning how it can sustain them, learning what it requires from them. Or as the title of Wendell Berry's essay in Wes Jackson's new *Anthology of Papers* goes, "Meeting the Expectations of the Land." If the matriarchs of our three or four or five ethnic groups can agree to meet the expectations of the land, then they've got something to begin to work from.

Putting the land first means reducing your hegemonial impulses to take away each other's territory, to agree on some equitability and reduce aggressive, competitive attempts to seize territory. Or even give territory back. It all sounds utopian, I'm sure. It's not a big idea, but Jesus, a lot of people have never thought of it—that we put the place first. We should put the place ahead of the U.S. flag, or ahead of our blackness or whiteness, or ahead of the fact that we speak English or Spanish, and then say, "The land is what comes first. Let's proceed from there."

JL   But the system of political boundaries seems to cloud the issue a lot.

GS   Well you know, ethnicity should not stand ahead of land or place. Ethnicity is second to place. Place comes first. Place comes ahead of class, too. I say this to the Marxists.

JL   I'd like to ask you to trace the evolution of anarchist thought from Kropotkin to the notion of bioregionalism.

GS   I'm not much of an anarchist historian, and so I'd have to kind of make it up. But anybody who has read *Mutual Aid*, Kropotkin's magnum opus, knows that he speaks many decades ahead of his time, as a kind of social ecologist. His insights into the virtues of indigenous cultures and into how natural systems work are way ahead of their time. His ideas do a huge end run around the Marxism of his day, so that the neo-Marxists following Rudolph Bahro are now proposing an ecologically sensitive Marxism—a Marxism which does not denigrate indigenous peoples.

In the meantime, what happened to anarchists? What happened to Kropotkin-type anarchists? I doubt that there is any continuous historical lineage, but there is a kind of semi-continuous, occasionally broken lineage that goes through the IWW, and miscellaneous bohemians, workers, writers, anthropologists, artists, radical scientists through the '20s to the '50s. Aldo Leopold, without knowing it. John Muir, without knowing it. Robinson Jeffers, sort of knowing it. D.H. Lawrence, sort of knowing it. Many streams of what often appeared to be irrelevant social and aesthetic thought nonetheless carried a certain torch of profound respect for the indigenous and for the natural—sometimes tagged with the word "romantic" or whatever, but surviving all those tags. It began to come together again, starting in the '50s, with the movement labeled "Beat," which was a real surfacing of ecological thought—though not so called—within American intellectual and aesthetic circles. So it's not an easily traceable history, but it's there.

The term "bioregionalism" came from people like Allen Van Newkirk and Peter Berg, and I suppose I gave it some energy—a kind of a fancy way of formalizing, giving a word to something that many of us have been doing all along—now we're making it coherent. The conditions of the 20th century make the importance of that coherence, the importance of that move, more evident to us. So it does become interesting to the ecologists, interesting to the political environmentalists, interesting to the Greens and the new Marxists, interesting to the fourth world people whose politics are involved in it. The call for "Bioregional Nations" is curious and kind of charming. And yet it's also obvious.

JL   A lot of people construe the term "anarchist" to be synonymous with "bomb-thrower," which is certainly not the case, and that's something that needs to be understood.

GS   Well, there was one line of people who called themselves anarchists in the 19th century who did specialize in terrorist acts targeted specifically at heads of state. That was one idea. I don't believe Kropotkin himself ever was involved in that or ever recommended it. We sometimes distinguish that kind of anarchism from philosophical anarchism. And the activist impulse can perhaps be understood in the way the Earth First! group is *defending territory, defending place.* That's what they're actually doing. They say, "We're defending wilderness," but they're defending place. They're defending place on the planet against, literally, outside interests, economic interests, using essentially nonviolent tactics. And their tactics would be understood and appreciated by centuries of people of the resistance. If you want to really go back, the anarchist resistance has always been there. Anarchism is not the absence of order. Anarchism is the assertion that social order comes from natural society, natural community, and natural culture, and is not the creation of the State. The State, which likes to talk about law and order, is actually entropic, and destroys order. It destroys the order of self-governing, self-maintaining, sustainable cultures. Stanley Diamond says all of history, in a sense, has been the unravelling of local cultures and local kinship groups and local sustainable, autonomous cultures by the spreading effects of the Imperium, of the dynamics of the metropole, the dynamics of world business cultures, starting way back with the Romans and before. Resistance through the centuries of Welsh and Breton, Manx, Scots, Basques, has been anarchist resistance. It's been the support of local order against imposed disorder.

JL   Conversations I've had with indigenous people have indicated how the relationship, the political interaction between the capitalist system and the Marxist system, has been imposed on people who have evolved within their own cultural context. And that's a big rub, because these larger political systems that have emerged from a dominant world culture are bent on placing their political systems before the sense of place and before the stewards of the place who have evolved within that particular environment. For instance, the tribal peoples who still live in America don't really know how to resist such a juggernaut. People like the Earth First! groups, who use nonviolent action in order to protect the sense of place, have begun to increase in number. Can you explain a bit more about how they regard themselves as protectors of place?

GS   Well, I don't know if they have defined themselves in quite that way. Because what Earth First! has been so far is a marvelously mobile strike force, based in the West and traveling to places throughout the West that are under imminent attack by mining or logging interests, whether on public land or private land. Generally their activities have been concerned with issues on public land—the commons—right now. As Earth First! wins more adherents throughout the West, people will take care of their own areas more, and the mobile strike force will not have to be quite so mobile. I would imagine it will continue to evolve from the way it is now, a fairly anarchistic organization with no real governance from the center, but simply a set of exciting working ideas on how to take care of things in your own place. So it can move from being a wilderness defense strike force, to a loose network of people who are based in various parts of the West, and the whole world, if you like, who come to a greater degree of self-consciousness about their involvement, commitment and responsibility to place, and then take action in place by legal means, or by illegal nonviolent means, if necessary, to demonstrate where the line is. To demonstrate how far you can go—how far these forces of capitalism, or industrial socialism can be allowed to go. So it is the activist spirit of Earth First! that is inspiring and useful to the self-preoccupied condition that comes over rural settlers sometimes. It teaches emerging bioregionalists, urban and rural people, how to get involved and do things. There is a very simple vow, which is: "I won't move. I'll stay here, love here." It doesn't have to be in the country; it doesn't have to be rural. It could be in a neighborhood in the suburbs, or a neighborhood in the inner city. If you take that vow, it doesn't mean you can't go on trips. It just means that you grow into the awareness that you are where you are and you're going to take responsibility for living there. That's where it all begins. That changes the politics around totally, if you have a rooted group of people who won't retreat.

EPILOGUE

OUR SPECIES has given mythic form to an intuitive understanding of humanity's place in Nature. Traditionally, mythic structures emerge from cultural interpretations of nature deities and the homelands over which they are presumed to preside. Humans inhabiting a given homeland attune their individual and collective organisms to deities whose presences are sensed to exist within natural forms. The divine essence of rock formations, mountain ranges, bodies of water, and nonhuman species is perceived and revered. This inherent spiritual sense provides a wisdom for humans who, recognizing the inevitability of death, define our role in life.

In Western culture the mythic process has been gradually subordinated by a collective refocusing on technology and scientific investigation. This great intellectual awakening is undoubtedly one of the most profound experiences in human history; indeed, it is regarded by many of the cerebrally oriented to be our species' *raison d'être*. For all the wonderful creativity generated by this rush of cultural evolution, it must be admitted that something precious is being lost. Our ability to intuit the sacred quality of life, to feel akin to other living creatures, to sense that we are actually part of the biosphere, is dangerously threatened.

Tsay Begeh Arch, Navajo Reservation, 1935

Television and computers have been major components in American culture for well over a generation. While it is true that TV puts us in instant contact with all corners of the planet and beyond, and computers have re-introduced a means of conceiving a system of factors in a state of simultaneity, an inherent bio-wisdom can be lost in the process of externalizing human attention through artificial intelligence. Bio-wisdom is a phenomenon whereby biota become equipped to respond to the environment and survive as part of the whole. Without the tempering influence of bio-wisdom, without the invocation of the intuitive processes inherent therein, purely objectified intelligence may program all biota into oblivion.

Western culture could be regarded as a monocultural tangent to the continuum of human history in which we have collectively focused on the human domination of Nature. This urge to dominate conceivably had its origins in the Fertile Crescent of antiquity. It was ratified in the biblical book of Genesis when the deity became anthropomorphised. Our proclivity for tool making gave physical form to our technofantasies. We finally industrialized in a burst of energy which altered our perception of reality and its meaning.

Other cultures which we tend to regard as archaic or primitive function in a context which has coordinates different from our own. This is illustrated by the way some cultures conceive of time. Time may be symbolized by a cross. The horizontal axis represents calendrical time—the time that applies to three-dimensional reality and is marked by the passage of the sun across the heavens. The vertical axis symbolizes spiritual refinement and broadening of scope using the entirety of the mental processes—the intellectual, intuitive, instinctive, emotional, sensory. Where the axes intersect is the center, the homeland of the whole human or the whole culture.

In order to elucidate the sacred nature of reality, humans assign symbolic significance to those aspects of reality which they perceive as sacred. These symbols and the way they are reiterated is the essence of the mythic process. Symbols are integrated by the cultural mind into comprehensible mythic structures that give meaning to the fact of existence; myths become a form of inner reality that richly embellishes the passage from birth to death. By comparing various mythic structures from different cultures throughout calendrical times one recognizes archetypal motifs that emerge again and again.

One pattern that seems ubiquitous is the recognition of the Earth as the Mother and the Sun as the Father. The Child of this union is Life. All living creatures possess an intelligence commensurate with their double helix. Time and again, the human role has been regarded as that of intermediary between the deities and the environment. The sense of stewardship that this implies has, in recent times, become a major tenet of the environmentalist ethic. It is ironic that it is from within this mythic construct that anthropocentrism had its genesis. It is also ironic that science, which promulgates technofantasy, has provided humans with an objectivity which allows us to comprehend that it is not *Homo sapiens* that resides at the center, but rather the biosphere. This knowledge raises metaphysical questions that place humans in a state of conflict, especially with regard to individual continuity.

Evidence suggests to me that individual consciousness ceases at the death of our corporeal forms. During our life spans, our corporeal forms are characterized by a combination of the genetic code inherent in our DNA molecules, and the sum of experiences—both inner and outer, as individuals or cultures or part of the total biotic mass—that happen to us in our passage through Life. If we have reproduced, we have contributed to the gene pool. Finally, when our corporeal forms cease to function, the atoms which comprise us are absorbed into other systems.

The important point is that we understand our relationship as humans to all other forms of biota. We are of the same stuff. Because we appear to be, at the moment, the most evolved species in the biotic community does not mean that we are Life's purpose. It would seem to me that the purpose of Life is a continuous evolution of consciousness and that *Homo sapiens* is merely a single point within Life's continuum. To the true egalitarian, all forms of Life are equal. Other Life forms, however, are not developing and detonating atomic bombs.

The present mode of human conduct endangers not only humankind, but the process of all Life. Since humans have caused the present biospheric catastrophe, humans must assume responsibility for relieving the biosphere of this awesome jeopardy. We need to identify the areas of human endeavor which imperil the biosphere and treat them as criminal acts. We must sophisticate a system of ethics sensitive to the entire biotic community. The ideal is that we bring our considerable array of mental and spiritual attributes into conscious focus to determine what factors must be acted upon to allow the planet to return to a state of biotic prosperity.

The first major hurdle for most humans to overcome is inertia, especially when facing problems of national or global magnitude. The human psyche is simply not expansive enough to include much beyond personal experience. In America, most of us (I hope) can at least visualize the general shape of the North American continent and with some modicum of effort determine the main geophysical characteristics—mountain ranges, plains, forested areas, deserts and *population centers*. If we take to heart the notion that human overpopulation and its ramifications are the leading causes of the planet's ills, and if we accept Garrett Hardin's premise that the carrying capacity of the land dictates the maximum human population, then humans must accept the onus for determining the *optimum* human population. This is a tall order because the list of factors seems endless.

However, if the landmass of a given continent is conceived of as an interrelated composite of *ecosystems* or watersheds, each of which is essentially self-sustaining if allowed to exist in the natural state, and if each of those ecosystems is examined closely, first its own characteristics and then how it integrates into the whole, the task seems merely monumental rather than impossible.

If this task were undertaken, criteria for establishing the human carrying capacity within a given ecosystem would have to be defined and evaluated. Cultural, intercultural and technological factors, current stage of environmental degradation, future probabilities based on knowledge of past human performance—this and much, much more would have to be factored into the criteria.

These criteria would be determined by regional committee members whose collective education, scientific and cultural expertise, sense of the land, intuition and insight are adequate for the task *and who are not biased in favor of growth for its own sake.*

Ecosystems are more intimately related than political systems. Political systems are composites of bureaucracies, whereas ecosystems are composites of geophysical features. Political systems are ephemeral; ecosystems are real.

ECOSYSTEMOLOGY should instantly become a part of the American elementary school curriculum, on a par with the three R's, in the hope that this aspect might become a model for other cultures, other nations. Without the collective understanding that the carrying capacity of the planet overrides economics, politics, religion, class distinctions—*even the presence of the human species*—the planet in its current aspect is about to be spent, utterly and frivolously.

Human population will have to diminish intelligently or perish miserably. Optimum human populations could be achieved *gradually* for each and every ecosystem on our continent. The carrying capacity of any ecosystem can be monitored by committee and maintained by consensus.

Currently, we in America comprise a culture with a pampered middle- and upper-class apparently committed to materialism. "Born to shop"—what a distinction!

Metropolitan areas such as New York City and Los Angeles, to say nothing of Tokyo and Mexico City, are unnaturally large concentrations of humans wherein natural balance is invisible. Ironically, it is mostly from within these megacenters of the "eco-ignorant" that the modern culture-bearers perpetrate the great technofantastic dream of materialism via advertising and media hype. Undoubtedly, these very megacenters will be the setting for forthcoming eco-disasters.

With depopulation must come decentralization—*gradually* and with growing understanding of the subordinate position of the human species to the overall biotic process. This may seem utopian, an impossible goal. Perhaps it is, but consider the alternative if the current juggernaut goes unchecked.

We have expended a disproportionately high ratio of the planet's resources celebrating human presence in the twentieth century. This means that we have to spend proportionately less as we wend our way out of our current and possibly final predicament.

At this point human overpopulation is a deadly reality. Soon it might no longer be a problem—if humans simply disappear because of famine, holocaust, pandemic or pollution. But alternatively, we may just veer into a course of balance, of ecosystemic planning, and thereby gradually realize that the planet comes first—it is the only planet we have and there are no other large-scale life crafts available to us now, and there never will be one as perfect for us as the one of which we are a part.

Let us understand the carrying capacity for what it is and oblige the urge to consciousness with discipline, temperance and joy.